W9-ACB-117

The Dramatic Difference

Drama in the Preschool and Kindergarten Classroom

Victoria Brown
and
Sarah Pleydell

Foreword by
Gavin Bolton

HEINEMANN
Portsmouth, NH

Heinemann
A division of Reed Elsevier Inc.
361 Hanover Street
Portsmouth, NH 03801–3912
http://www.heinemann.com

Offices and agents throughout the world

The authors and publisher wish to thank those who have generously given permission to reprint borrowed material:

Portions of Chapter 8, "Assessment" originally appeared as "Assessment of Preschool Drama Programs" by Victoria Brown. *The Drama Theatre Teacher,* Vol. 4, No. 3. Reprinted by permission of the American Alliance for Theatre & Education.

Excerpts from *Singing to the Monster: A Teacher's Guide to Using Dramatic Play for the Resolution of Children's Anger and Tension* by Victoria Brown and Sarah Pleydell. Copyright 1994 by The Kay Fund for Children. Used by permission of The Kay Fund for Children.

Library of Congress Cataloging-in-Publication Data
Brown, Victoria (Victoria L.)
    The dramatic difference : drama in the preschool and kindergarten
  classroom / Victoria Brown and Sarah Pleydell ; [editor, Lisa A. Barnett].
       p.   cm.
    Includes bibliographical references.
    ISBN 0–325–00121–9 (alk. paper)
    1. Drama in education. 2. Play. 3. Early childhood education—
  Activity programs. I. Pleydell, Sarah. II. Barnett, Lisa A.
  III. Title.
PN3171.B76 1999
372.13'32—dc21   99-25827
                                                                              CIP

Editor: Lisa A. Barnett
Production: Denise Warner/Colophon
Cover design: Darci Mehall
Cover art: Cynthia Matsakis
Manufacturing: Louise Richardson

Printed in the United States of America on acid-free paper
03 02 01 00 99   DA   1 2 3 4 5

*This book is dedicated to our children,
Nicholas, Michael, Thomas, Ellie,
Justice and True.*

Contents

Foreword

GAVIN BOLTON

Victoria Brown and Sarah Pleydell are not only gifted teachers of young children ages 3 to 6, they have a flair for making what they do accessible to their readers. To say that this book is about drama is to mislead and understate. For it is about children and the way they learn when their imaginations are tapped; and it is about the school curriculum. Drama is the process through which children engage with that curriculum. This is not a book on how "nice" drama is as a vehicle for "self-expression," for "fun," for "letting off steam," for "rehearsing lines," or for "facing an audience of applauding parents." This is a serious text on cognitive development through drama that should be studied by all teachers in training, by all teachers of young children, and by all educators. For the "as if" mode of mental behavior, naturally adopted by most children in their play, can be harnessed for curriculum ends.

Have you noticed how much satisfaction children get through engaging a parent in their play? And how an astute parent can use occasions of heightened imagination subtly to drop in extra information, extend the range of vocabulary, or pose a problem? The authors have developed a pedagogic style that harnesses this special child/parent teaching moment by establishing that the teacher is a necessary part of the class' dramatic invention.

Of course there are times in their wide range of vivid examples when the class spontaneously takes the invention out of the teacher's hands altogether, but such instances are as rare as they are precious. For the most part, the teacher should—indeed *must*—operate *from within* the fiction to focus on the learning objective, to ask the questions that challenge the children to think just that bit harder, to gently bring in the child who might be left out or who hangs back, to insist on respectful listening to the child who whispers rather than shouts, to check that they have understood a new concept, to be a model for heightened language.

The secret of the effectiveness of this "teacher in role," as it is commonly called, is that it is the teacher's *adopted* role that focuses, that asks questions, that draws in, that insists, that checks and models, which is all part of this fiction. Thus the regular teacher functions become *contextualized*. It is "as if" they have emerged naturally from the fictitious world they have all been making together, as if the fiction *needed* them.

Such a teaching aid brings an *extra* dimension to teaching and learning—an extra dimension, not an alternative one—for, in a curious way, when the teacher comes out of "role" and behaves just like a teacher again, that normal function becomes enhanced as though the tacit understanding the children and teacher have shared in their combined fiction making now continues to reflect their regular interactions.

Victoria Brown and Sarah Pleydell make it very clear that when the teacher takes on a role, it is not a full-blown character. The role is but an indicator and must be no more than that. What the children are seeing is their teacher *and* the role, at the same time. This "double reading" is the definitive feature of make-believe play. Jean Piaget's observation of children at play demonstrated the child's natural ability to both slide a shell along the edge of a box and see it as a cat on the wall at the same time. The child knows it is a shell as well as "knowing" it as a cat. Here is the very basis of learning to read and handle numbers, commanding the prereading skill of connecting sign and meaning.

In leading the drama the teacher is operating a duality of role, about which the authors give excellent advice. If the teacher gets carried away with her own acting prowess, it may backfire. The authors give an example of how some very young children screamed when a teacher put on a witch's hat and assumed a convincing witchlike voice. What this teacher failed to do was to invite the class to advise her on how she should best "sign" witch and then carry out the children's suggestions, apologizing for "not being very good at it." In other words, very young children must feel they have control and that they are "making" the teacher's role.

In my long career, I have never come across such an astonishing range of props (visual, auditory, olfactory, and kinesthetic "signs") as can be found in this record of work. Victoria and Sarah have an instinct for finding just the right indicator, inductor, or stimulus for entry into a make-believe world. Their classroom is a place where children are more than themselves. They quote from Lev Vygotski who says that dramatic play makes children "ten feet tall." Their skilled eyes embrace both the needs of the whole group, filled with shared wonder as a black-gloved hand becomes a spider many-legging its way across the carpet, and also the need of the individual who needs protecting, encouraging, or just leaving alone. From early on in their introduction to drama they establish a safe place in the form of their circle. It is their starting point, and great journeys can be experienced there—as they put it, "They travel thousands of miles without moving from their spot." It can be departed from in adventure, but it is always there to return to: it is home. They may return to it as part of a quiet narration, or because the music guides them back—or simply because the lunch tables are being set and concentration has been lost!

Yes, there is wonder and magic in this classroom, but Victoria and Sarah know that the inner core of their creativity is that focus on the curriculum. The teacher adapts the material to meet her choice of curricular objective. She sometimes cleverly uses the device of inventing a character who has to be "taught" by the children. For example, in one case they are visited by an "alien," who, they discover, does not understand the five senses, and so they set about teaching her! They are continually weaving two worlds, two kinds of knowledge, that of myth and of science. They want their classes to know more about history, geography, math, botany, physics, and health as a direct result of experiencing the dramatic form. They want them to be better readers, better listeners, better sharers—because they have the experience of the dramatic form.

Thus the drama made in the classroom cannot be considered in isolation. It is an integral part of the whole learning curriculum and indeed of the whole school day. The map they are studying may be of the journey they are making in their drama; the drawing or writing they are doing may be the village constitution, the rules for which evolved in their drama. Their talking may be about some issue that cropped up that has to be resolved. They may all crouch around a large piece of writing that they are struggling to read—and it *must* be read because it carries an important message about the secret treasure—and they can't get on with their drama until they grasp its contents.

There is so much to learn about education from this enlightened book. The authors can be trusted, because they are genuine practitioners and their ideas are well tested. Their chapter on assessment is a model of common sense, in which they recognize public expectations while warning about the limitations of trying to measure matters that work at such a fundamental level of learning. But I think the biggest appeal of the book to the reader will be the astonishingly varied verbal illustrations. When you read them, you are *there*. My wife caught me smiling as I read. "Is that book funny?" she asked. My smile was not a response to humor. It was a smile of *recognition*—and anyone who knows anything about the classroom of young children will smile with me.

Preface

Nicholas is three years old. He is playing "doctor" in the housekeeping area of his preschool classroom with David. "What's wrong?" asks David, the doctor.

Lying on the floor curled up with his hands on his belly, Nicholas responds in a dramatic voice, "I have a baby in my tummy."

"What's the baby doing in there?"

"Kicking me."

"Why?"

"He wants to come out and be my brother," Nicholas replies. The teacher, who has been observing from a distance brings over a stethoscope, "Doctor, could you use this stethoscope?" she inquires. The two boys continue their play, debating whether it is kicking or heartbeats they hear. Nicholas is using dramatic play to explore the events evolving at home with a new baby on the way and his own changing role.

There is a consensus among most early childhood educators that young children learn best through two key experiences: dramatic play and interaction with their environment. Yet even within the wide range of educational and day-care settings, curricular priorities rarely reflect this consensus. One problem is that, with a growing number of curricular demands for young children, there is little time in the school day for play. Day-care settings may be less structured, but many cannot provide the space and variety of materials to stimulate a broad range of experiences for play and active learning. For these reasons, many under-funded educational and day-care facilities can restrict rather than foster early childhood learning (Robinson et al. 1997; Phillips 1987).

Fortunately, young children's imaginations are unlimited. This is why drama, engaging the child's imagination, serves as an excellent learning medium. By creating experiences through teacher-led drama work, space can be transformed through the imagination. Teaching through drama can also maximize the use of time, incorporating curricular goals while providing opportunity for play and experiential learning.

Classroom drama offers a vital bridge between dramatic play and teacher-initiated learning. It can compensate for the shortcomings of poor facilities and scant materials, by creating an environment in which interactive learning is only as restricted as the imagination itself.

Preschool and kindergarten children, whose learning is primarily the product of experience and interaction within their environment, would arguably have the most to gain from drama (particularly at ages three to four when language development is still occurring at a rapid pace). Yet preschool children are the least likely to receive drama instruction. When the arts are included in preschool and kindergarten classrooms it is primarily music and visual arts, though it could be argued that drama and dance are better suited to the physical–gestural nature of early childhood learning (Cazden 1981; Piaget 1962, 1974; Bryant 1974; Kolb 1984; Gardner 1985). This is particularly discouraging in light of the growing need for appropriate and effective programming at the preschool level. More children than ever before are attending preschool or some child-care program (approximately thirteen million), many for a full ten-hour day (Phillips 1987; Robinson et al. 1997).

One obstacle is that arts programming mandated for the schools does not necessarily apply to preschool programs, or even kindergarten. Many preschool programs and most day-care centers are run outside of the public school system. Even if a preschool were part of a school system that benefited from a drama program, age appropriate drama experiences would not be guaranteed, partly because most drama-in-education specialists have not been trained to work with children as young as three and four. Kindergarten classes frequently miss out on these opportunities as well, particularly half-day programs. Furthermore, there are few resources available for the preschool or kindergarten teacher committed to providing quality drama experiences to students. Most college courses in educational drama, as well as drama texts and how-to books, ordinarily exclude children under the age of five. Given the developmental differences of younger children, major adaptations would be needed.

The aim of this book is to help redress this imbalance in the pedagogy of early childhood and drama-in-education:

- Drama is presented as a dynamic learning medium for preschool and kindergarten children that accommodates curricular demands while nurturing the need for play and active learning.
- Strategies are introduced for leading curricular-based drama work that will also facilitate the goals of child development.

- Age-appropriate drama sessions that integrate these strategies are described in detail, including teachers' choices, children's responses, and vice versa.
- Additional suggestions are outlined for developing new drama work, and there is a step-by-step guide for planning drama "from scratch."
- Recommendations are also made for integrating multisensory experiences into the drama and for adapting dramatic activity to accommodate children with special needs.

Most important, this book is designed as a resource for teachers and drama specialists, highlighting ways they can efficiently and effectively maximize the drama experience in the preschool and kindergarten classroom.

Acknowledgments

We are blessed to have had the support of our families and the counsel of colleagues. While our children taught us about play and the power of unrestrained imagination, our husbands, Christofer Zachariadis and Jim Tom Haynes, encouraged us to stay on task and provided the space and time to be creative and productive. Friends and colleagues listened to our ideas, read drafts of the manuscript, and contributed valuable suggestions. We are particularly grateful for the contributions of Rachel Briley, Julie Zachariadis, Janice McKelvey, Mimi Flaherty, and the Wolf Trap Institute for Early Learning Through the Arts. We are equally grateful to many teachers in schools across the country who have shared their classrooms, time, ideas, energy, and insights, as we tested our work. We want to especially mention the staff of the School for Friends, Prince George's County Head Start, Rosemary Hills Elementary School, Oyster Bilingual Elementary, and the brave teachers who became involved in the Singing to the Monster project.

Introduction

Imagination: The Dramatic Connection

Have you ever imagined that you are somebody else, or that someone else is with you? Certainly you've imagined being somewhere else, perhaps in some exotic setting, boating down the Amazon or strolling along a beach in Tangier?

Young children's lives are steeped in this kind of imaginary experience. Yet, for them, there is much more to imagining than just seeing or hearing something within the privacy of their own minds. They cannot easily separate what they are thinking from what they are doing and, therefore, their imaginative thought will often spontaneously erupt into dramatic action. This externalization of imagination through dramatic action begins to occur at around ten months and evolves into dramatic play—acting out an imagined situation alone or in collaboration with one or more other children.[1]

Most of us have at least distant memories of using our imagination in this way. Some may even recall imaginary friends. For many of us there are still moments where imaginative thought carries over into dramatic action, such as talking out loud, gesturing to imagined persons or swaying to imagined music. This might take the form of the vivid recollection of past experiences or the envisioning of new ones.

As adults, we also use our imaginations daily to facilitate problem solving, contemplate possibilities, relate to another person's point of view, or empathize with someone else's plight. This capacity to imagine ourselves in various situations—to think "as if"—is an essential ingredient to realizing our individual potential and creating successful relationships with others.[2]

Dramatic Play and Early Development

Young children, largely through their dramatic play, are developing their "as if" perspective toward the world around them. The ability to think "as if," along with other aspects of dramatic play, has been linked to cognitive development and the formation of social and interpersonal skills. For decades, there has been a significant amount of research and attention paid to the role of play, specifically dramatic play, as it relates to child development. Through dramatic play, children solve problems, express emotions, develop critical thinking skills, and engage in socialization. Indeed, play is a primary means by which children develop a sense of self (Haight and Miller 1993).

ACTIVE LEARNING

As Piaget describes, the child's primary mode of learning is through physical interaction with their environment. Learning through action is a prerequisite to learning through language or learning through thought. In the early years, interaction with the environment occurs primarily through play and imitation. A child imitates what she sees or experiences in order to assimilate new information (Piaget 1962, 1974; and Vygotsky).

"You be the mommy and I'll be the pizza man," says four year old Michael to his playmate, adding, "and you be 'fustated' cause I'm late." The symbolic substance of dramatic play ranges from fire fighter or doctor role play wherein children aspire to mastery of the adult world, to situations in which their play relates to subjects of personal significance (such as a new sibling or a parent returning to work outside the home). These subjects will usually be repeated frequently in the child's play as a means of mastering an understanding of the issue (Garvey 1990, Henddrick 1992, Ounce of Prevention Fund 1996).

SUPPORTING RESEARCH

Until recently, the importance of interaction with the environment through play on a young child's development has been recognized primarily through observational studies (Piaget 1962; and Vygotsky 1978). Since the mid 1990s, however, more direct evidence has emerged, correlating brain development to the amount of a child's physical interaction and sensory experiences. Neuroscientists have discovered, for example, that base patterns of memory form as children experience their sensory environment in greater and greater detail. Children continue to elaborate and modify this patterning throughout their lives. It is significant, however, that they acquire ninety percent of these base patterns within the first five years of life, creating a template on which future learning is attached (Hannaford 1995, Gazzaniga 1995, Damasio 1994).

Dramatic Play and Early Childhood Education

In most schools and day-care settings, there is generally an area set aside for dramatic play, and most curricula for preschool and kindergarten emphasize an active learning approach. Yet a close examination of these programs, particularly kindergarten settings, will indicate that there is little time allotted in the daily routine for free play. This problem is most prevalent in kindergarten, where teachers often feel pressured to cover too much material in too little time (Jones and Reynolds 1992).

This may be a consequence of an overcrowded curriculum and the back-to-basics movement. Yet, in view of recent discoveries about the correlation of sensory experiences to early brain development—and hence the importance of active learning—getting back to the basics of play may indeed be a more effective approach for early childhood education (Kostelnik, Soderman and Whiren 1993; Shipley 1993).

The Dramatic Difference

Like dramatic play, drama is experiential in nature, involving imitation, practice, and repetition and engaging the whole child. Both involve the senses, cognition, emotion, and movement—creating a vivid imprint. Drama can even function as a segue, integrating dramatic play with teacher-initiated learning and optimizing the educational potential of valuable class time.

Dramatic Play and Classroom Drama

It is within this context that drama is presented in this book—active learning for young children. It is important to understand that we do not propose that young children engage in drama as a performance art. Classroom drama is process oriented. Presenting plays with young children is not recommended, particularly in a formal setting.[3]

We advocate the use of drama to create learning experiences, ranging from spontaneous drama initiated by a child's curiosity to drama work that is planned and guided by a teacher with specific educational objectives in mind.

TERMINOLOGY

The following terminology is used throughout the book:

Dramatic play: In dramatic play children pretend to be someone else or pretend to be themselves in imagined situations.

Drama, process drama, and drama work: These terms refer to

process-oriented drama with children—not presentation, but exploration of ideas and situations through drama. In many ways, drama
is teacher-guided dramatic play. Other terms used in the field refer
to this use of drama as *creative drama, child drama,* or *drama-in-
education.*

Dramatic activity: categories or types of drama experiences, for example, creative movement, improvisation, and so on (see Chapter 1).

Drama session: a sequence of dramatic activity in which children
create an imaginary environment, situation, and characters experience and explore. This sequence may be spontaneous or planned.
Most drama sessions described in this book continue for twenty to
forty-five minutes.

Extended drama: drama work that requires several sessions to
complete.

Drama experience: the individual or group experience created by
the drama. Each child's encounter will be unique, and the same sequence of dramatic activity repeated (with the same or a different
group) will create a different and distinct group experience.

Play: generally refers to dramatic play as defined earlier. *Play* is
never used in this book to mean theatre performance of any kind.

Teacher: any adult caring for or working with children, including
drama specialists.

Class, classroom: any setting where children ages three to six are
cared for, including the wide range of day-care facilities.[4]

Drama and Early Childhood Development

According to the National Association for the Education of Young Children (NAEYC), the early childhood curriculum should address five categories of child development: social, emotional, physical, cognitive, and
creative (Bredekamp 1997). Drama can be a highly effective tool for supporting each of these categories, either naturally or through well-defined
objectives.[5]

SOCIAL DEVELOPMENT

Those who have eavesdropped on a group of young children deeply engaged in dramatic play have a sense of the broad range of social skills
being exercised. A teacher-led drama session creates the same kind of
environment, with a clear focus on teacher determined objectives. Interaction, negotiation, and cooperation are critical components of the process. In "The Stranger" (an extended drama in Chapter 3), preschool

children create a village, including individual and shared housing and a well-debated constitution. The constitution reflects their own needs and concerns within the social setting of the real classroom.

EMOTIONAL DEVELOPMENT

Drama facilitates emotional development by creating an ambiance that inspires children to express and explore their feelings. In the symbolic world of make-believe, children often express thoughts and concerns that would otherwise go undiscovered or remain repressed. As one four-year-old girl noted after an energetic enactment of Maurice Sendack's story, *Where the Wild Things Are,* "I feel better now, my head's all cleared up inside."

PHYSICAL DEVELOPMENT

Drama and creative movement activities can be structured to develop and practice gross and fine motor control and to promote strength and flexibility. Activity, such as manipulating props, using finger-play and finger puppets, and miming various hand tasks, exercises fine motor control. Gross motor skills are reinforced through various creative movement activities described in this book, such as children enacting the wind, wild ponies, caterpillars, and jumping frogs.

COGNITIVE DEVELOPMENT

Any form of process drama, be it spontaneous dramatic play or teacher-led drama work, is attuned to the way in which young children learn. In drama, as in play, cognition evolves from the physical exploration and understanding of a concept to its mental representation, and finally its verbal expression. After participating in a dramatization of *Where the Wild Things Are*, children's descriptive language explodes as they compare their imaginative versions of "Wild Things" with pictorial representations in the book, keenly noting differences in color, size, shape, and even affect.[6]

CREATIVE DEVELOPMENT

"Where does snow come from?" asks three and a half-year-old Nikki, after a drama session exploring winter. "Where do *you* think snow comes from?" replies her teacher. After a thoughtful pause, Nikki responds, "I think it's leftover clouds that God crumbles up and throws down for people to play with."

Through creative problem solving, creative movement, or the spontaneity of an improvisation, drama engages children's imaginations and stretches their creative thinking. Such programs are especially appropriate for young children. Indeed, most educational research in the arts indicates that when creativity is developed at an early age, its benefits are continual and are transferred to many intellectual tasks (Getzels and Jackson 1962; Goals 2000 Arts Education Partnership 1998).[7]

Drama and the Curriculum

In addition to its intrinsic value, drama can be used as a medium for learning across the curriculum. It can tap into virtually endless content, yet it has the capacity not only to deepen the children's understanding of that content, but also to discover and define their own relationship to it.

LANGUAGE ARTS

Language arts is at the core of most early childhood curricula and is the subject with the most obvious connection to drama. Indeed, language arts and drama comprise the same skills: speaking, listening, reading, and writing. Drama has the capacity to stir a child's curiosity and provoke questions and idea sharing. One five-year-old boy, waving his hand frantically after an extended drama, remarked, "I've got so many questions inside my head they're gonna fly away if I don't ask them right now!"

At the earliest age, a child learns language by practice, and drama can create a strong stimulus for the use and practice of language in a natural and spontaneous environment. Playing a variety of roles provides children the opportunity to experiment with various levels and uses of language. A teacher-guided drama session can be structured to encourage such variance, bearing in mind the specific language skills needed, including speech and literacy.

SOCIAL STUDIES AND SCIENCE

Young children discover their place in the world by observing the people around them—at home, in the classroom and the community, and also through books and media. In the preschool curriculum, social studies and science are usually informal, covering basic elements of social awareness, living things, and the environment. This is expanded in kindergarten to cover children's awareness of the variety of roles and cultural differences in their world, ethics, and celebrated historical events and persons. Science often overlaps with these social issues. Young children are introduced to the needs of people and other living things, and they are encouraged to contemplate the effect of people's behavior on the environment.

These and other aspects of social studies and science provide excellent content for drama work. Advancing children's comprehension of the links between their own lives and the larger community they inhabit requires more than just discussion. In drama, children are encouraged not only to play with the ideas presented by the teacher, but also to feel what is happening and to understand what it means. In the theme-based drama "The Stranger," children spend time creating a village community so that when the homeless stranger arrives on the scene, they are deeply invested in the experience. This investment motivates "the villagers" to verbally express their emotions, ideas, and opinions and to respond to those of others. Through the drama they are able to see an issue from various perspectives.

MATH AND LOGICAL THINKING

Like social studies and science for preschool and kindergarten children, math encompasses basic skills such as counting and how numbers relate to children's lives. Although this book does not present a drama session specifically focused on using math skills, there are activities integrated in several dramas that require children to use math skills, such as counting—adding up Sky Woman's babies in the *Sky Woman* story; measurement—figuring the ingredients for a loaf of bread in *The Giant Jam Sandwich* (Chapter 2), then multiplying those figures to create the recipe for the enormous loaf that is needed; problem solving—deciding how many water containers the astronauts must take on their journey to the moon; and the varied use of size and space—creating a map of the young boy's journey in *The Mud Pony* (Chapter 2). You can design a drama to emphasize math skills if this is one of your objectives.

Developmental Differences

If you have experience leading process drama with older children and have tried using similar methodology with preschool children or even kindergartners, the developmental differences become clear early on, particularly with children ages three and four. The most significant differences that affect planning and leading drama with this group are the following:

1. Young children generally have a much shorter attention span than do older children and are more easily distracted. Furthermore, most children at this age have not yet mastered physical

control. This is particularly true in a group setting, such as a circle-time activity. Turn taking or long periods of listening to the teacher present is particularly challenging.

2. Young children engaged in dramatic play easily slip back and forth between fantasy and reality. This holds true even when there is a high level of emotional involvement, such as a child in role as an angry dragon slayer, or a doctor taking care of a sick baby. An interruption from a parent or sibling does not seem to affect that child's ability to momentarily leave then slip right back into intense dramatic action.

3. When a young child is engaged in dramatic play, there is often a genuine sense of reality and emotional involvement in the pretend world. This is very different from an older child, who is always aware that the scene is pretend. The older child knows that the sword in hand and dragon are merely props. But the younger knight believes, for that moment anyway, that the stick is indeed a real sword that has slain a real dragon, which may only be a pillow.

4. In a group setting, young children tend to imitate and/or defer to the loudest voices in the group, making genuine group consensus hard to achieve.

5. Experiences and language use are generally more limited, requiring more direction and guidance from the teacher (Cazden 1981).

Making Drama Age Appropriate

To address these developmental differences when preparing and leading drama work for preschool and kindergarten children, the following accommodations are recommended:

1. Structure the drama as a series of short segments.
2. Use repetition to reinforce new language and concepts.
3. Encourage children to imitate as a starting point.
4. Clarify the distinction between reality and fantasy.
5. Begin the drama with a clear introduction and end with a closing.
6. Introduce techniques to maintain control and focus.
7. Provide opportunity for individual contributions.

STRUCTURING THE DRAMA INTO SEGMENTS

To accommodate young children's short attention spans, build in frequent opportunities within the drama to regroup. This may be necessary as often as every five or ten minutes, especially for three- and early four-year-old children. No matter how long the overall session may be, it should consist of a series of short activities that build on each other.

It is also helpful to vary the level and type of activity from scene to scene, providing for an occasional opportunity for gross motor activity, while maintaining the children's focus. For example, if children are dramatizing the story of *Where the Wild Things Are,* and have been parading around the room creating "rumpus," Max's journey home could be done quietly sitting in a circle, miming the boat ride back home. Sequence the activity, building from imitation and simple movement to a more complex dramatic activity that requires choice, decision making, and problem solving.

PROVIDING FOR REPETITION

Repetition is important at this age to reinforce new concepts. Repetition allows children to become more comfortable with movement or dialogue, and it builds self-confidence. More important, through the process of repetition, young children create and add intricacy to their imaginative pictures, establishing new nerve paths in the memory (Hannaford 1995).

Select important words and motions, or a sequence of events, that can be repeated within a drama session. A sequence of three repetitions is common in myth, folk, and fairy tales and also works well in drama. By the third sequence, children are usually quite confident and eager to show what will happen next. Many children's books use repetition in this way and make good selections for story dramatization.

Variations can be built into repetition to maintain interest and encourage creative thinking. In "Heavy Elephants and Light Butterflies" (Chapter 7), a tissue is dropped, floating to the floor, and children copy the movement several times, first with their hands, then their heads, shoulders, backs, and even bottoms. Each time they follow the tissue movement, the concept of "lightness" is transferred to different body parts (kinesthetic learning). Eventually they will be able to generalize this new concept to comprehending the lightness of a butterfly's movement.

ALLOWING FOR IMITATION

Imitation is critical as a component of dramatic play and to the developing thought process of the young child. Through imitating the actions, sounds, and language of one's environment, comprehension of self in relation to one's world grows in capacity and complexity. Through this process, which begins in infancy, imitation serves as a starting place for the development of imagination and creative thought.[8]

It is natural for young children to imitate the teacher as well as their peers. Imitation is certainly appropriate for the beginning of a drama session, especially for those too shy to participate on their own. Modeling a particular movement or use of language allows the teacher to expand the children's repertoire. Eventually children can be encouraged to try something different: a different way of dancing like a giraffe, or making their bodies float and glide like a leaf.

DISTINGUISHING REALITY FROM FANTASY

Those of us who have used puppets in the classroom are aware of children's ability to completely believe in and interact with the puppet as if it were real. Young children similary accept the teacher in role, sometimes actually believing she is a different person. For this reason, teachers should establish clear transitions between their teacher and drama roles.

Children at this age are also able to switch back and forth between roles in drama (varying gender) and are comfortable with everyone in the class playing the same role simultaneously. Simultaneous role play allows all children to experience the role of protagonist and sustains ongoing participation (see Chapter 1 for suggestions on roles for children and teachers).

CREATING A CLEAR INTRODUCTION AND CLOSING

Although children themselves are continually moving back and forth between reality and fantasy, the teacher needs to establish which mode is dominant at any given time. In drama and dramatic play time, fantasy is the predominant world, and in classroom time, reality is. These transitions must be made clear. Before jumping into the drama work, establish a routine that signals the beginning of drama time.

A well defined closing routine for each drama session is also important, facilitating the transition from the drama world back to the reality of the classroom. The closure should be designed to help children understand that the drama is over, calm them down, reflect on their work, and prepare them for the next activity. Information and ideas on introducing and closing a drama are described in Chapter 1.

MAINTAINING CONTROL AND FOCUS

A major misconception is that imaginative play is a free-for-all. Teachers of young children often avoid trying drama for fear of losing control of the class. Children do need a certain amount of freedom within a drama session, but limits can easily be established, such as creating a sign or hand symbol for signaling the children to return to the circle. Multisensory props can also be used to capture (and recapture) their focus and enhance learning (see Chapter 4).

Children's ability to maintain focus is directly related to the amount and quality of their participation in the drama session. Ongoing participation can be accomplished by alternating action-oriented activity with seated participation, such as miming the action or continuing the scenario using hand puppets or sign play, and by limiting observation and turn taking. There are several suggestions described in Chapter 4 and Chapter 7 (and demonstrated within the various dramas) for keeping children focused and involved.

PROVIDING FOR INDIVIDUAL CONTRIBUTIONS

The teacher must build in opportunities for individual children to express their ideas and ask questions that allow their creative input to flesh out and direct the evolving plan. When problem solving, integrate as many suggestions from the children as possible, encouraging those least likely to speak out. Whether he's naming a color, feeling, or flower, each child deserves a chance to be heard.

When a teacher does present a problem to a group—for example, "How shall we get out of this whale?"—make sure not only to give all children an opportunity to talk, but also to encourage originality: "Ben's idea is to tickle the whale, can you come up with something different?" If taking time for each child to share becomes problematic, work separately with small groups of three to five children, or switch media to encourage individual expression. In *Brave Irene* (Chapter 2), children are asked to design a party dress for the Duchess. There are many different swatches of fabric, so each child can select their own and explain what makes it a good choice.

Using This Book

Success in using drama with preschool and kindergarten children depends primarily on the value that the classroom teacher sees in such work, and on that teacher's ability to create opportunities for drama. As with using any new teaching method, beginning efforts may result in disappointment and discouragement. Keep in mind that both teacher and children are experimenting with new roles and new rules for the classroom. The teacher must clarify for the students that boundaries permitted for drama do not necessarily carry over for other classroom activities.

Throughout this book you will find descriptions of drama sessions and extended drama work, ranging from spontaneous to preplanned, that actually occurred in preschool and kindergarten classrooms. These reports detail teachers' choices and children's responses and vice versa. Perhaps they can be viewed as case studies, illustrating a variety of methods (Chapter 1) and the age-appropriate strategies described earlier.

Instead of viewing these drama sessions as "lesson plans" to be copied step by step, our hope is that you will extrapolate from these shared experiences ideas and methods to apply to your own classroom style and curricula goals. Your choices and your students' responses will be different from the choices made by the teachers leading these sessions and the responses and choices of their students. To spark your own creativity, we have included suggestions for creating new dramas. These "outlines" are intended as the next step—maps to help you find your own way.

In the back of this book you will find a bibliography. It lists each drama session and recommends follow-up titles of children's literature. Many of these make good resources for further dramatization. Refer to the Table of Contents for a comprehensive list of all the information you will need to locate each activity (titles, page numbers, and age group information).

If you are trying drama for the first time, you may want to begin by creating fixed lesson plans, then, as confidence builds, allow for more choice and spontaneity from the children. Being open to the children's responses can be frightening, but it's well worth doing so while building up your risk-taking skills. When you feel grounded in the methodology, we invite you to return to the section on planning drama (Chapter 1). This provides a framework for developing your own material, based on the interests and unique needs of the individual classes you teach.

Children do not simply acquire a series of skills that are taught by parents and teachers—they *emerge* as communicators, problem solvers, and humanitarians through holistic experiences. Drama is perhaps unique in this way as a multidimensional medium for early childhood learning. Perhaps this is because drama has the potential for communicating to young children in their own language: the language of make-believe. In this world, "gesture and mime—language in movement . . . is the real social language of the child" (Piaget 1955, 71). Drama links "language in movement" with spoken language, creating a bridge between the physical world and the spoken word. Moreover, it introduces young minds to "as if" symbolic thinking, the intellectual foundation for problem solving, social learning, and even reading.

Finally, young children learn through drama because it is participatory and because it is fun. In early childhood education, where young minds are just beginning their journey into the realm of formal education and where teachers have so much to teach in so little time, learning through drama makes sense.[9]

Notes

1. Several excellent resources provide a more detailed account of dramatic play in early childhood, including: Garvey (1990), Fein and Rivkin (1986), Paley (1990), Piers (1972), and Piaget (1962).

2. Jerome Singer further describes the importance of the child's "as if" perspective in *The Child's World of Make-Believe*. See also Sara Smilansky and E. Klugman, editors of *Children's Play and Learning*, and Richard Courtney's *The Dramatic Curriculum*.

3. The misery of playing a duck, or a tree in the school play when everyone really wants to be the princess or the knight, or the embarrassment of parents laughing in the wrong places, or not able to attend, are examples of the many anxieties that outweigh the potential benefits of young children performing.

4. Considering that many children do reach the age of six before leaving kindergarten, we have included children up to age six in our preschool and kindergarten category.

5. For information on theory and research documenting the value of dramatic play and classroom drama for young children, see Smilansky and Shefatya (1990), Wittmer and Honig (1994), Salazar et al. (1993), Christie and Johnsen (1983), Piers (1972), Fromberg (1990), Vygotsky (1967), Slade (1954), Way (1967), Courtney (1974), Bergen (1988), Fein and Rivkin (1986).

6. It is generally agreed that visual/spatial and physical/kinesthetic modes of communication are more easily perceived, retained, and produced by young children than are oral/aural communication. Howard Gardner's theory of multiple intelligences supports this notion, suggesting that each of these modes of communication (bodily/kinesthetic, spatial, and linguistic) constitutes a separate symbol system, perceived and processed in different areas of the brain. Drama utilizes those symbol systems that might be considered more compatible with young children's thought processes (Gardner 1985).

7. Some educators have recognized the importance of drama and other arts in the curriculum. The Wolf Trap Institute for Early Learning Through the Arts has been a pioneer in this effort, specializing in using arts with preschool children and teacher training around the country since 1981. More recently, National Head Start Bureau added a requirement in their 1998 Head Start Program Performance Standards that all Head Start programs serving children from birth to age five must be "Ensuring opportunities for creative self-expression through activities such as art, music, movement, and dialogue." Related guidelines recommend

that "Children need to express themselves creatively. Their experiences with art, music, drama, dance, creative movement, and related conversation enhance their overall development." Suggestions include "stimulating imagination through drama and other language-rich experiences" (U.S. Department of Health and Human Services 1998).

8. Imitation has been investigated extensively by Jean Piaget and experimentally studied by social-learning theorists. In addition to being considered an important component of the learning process, it is generally accepted as a primary mode for acquisition of social behavior.

9. For information regarding formal research examining drama in preschool and kindergarten education see the following: Adamson (1981), Brown (1990), Goodman (1991), Haley (1978), Hensel (1973), Linfield (1996), Marbach and Yawkey (1980), Page (1983), Pettigrew (1994), Pipkin and DiMenna (1989), Saltz and Johnson (1977), Tucker (1971), and Wolf (1996).

Getting Started

The Nature of Dramatic Activity

Most of the dramatic activity in this book was developed to help children experience and explore a new story, concept, or theme introduced by the teacher, or in response to their expressed interest. There is generally a progression within a drama session, beginning with introductory activities, which allow children to explore and/or develop the characters and the setting of the imaginary world they are creating. This is followed by dramatic activity, which moves or builds the action, or "storyline," as if the children are living through the experience being created. If the activity provides for spontaneity, children can become engrossed, the same way they are in their natural dramatic play—not only truly believing, but also creating the moment.

Dramatic activity can be organized along a four-way continuum (as illustrated in the following diagram) with child-initiated to teacher-initiated dramatic activity defining one axis and spontaneous and structured dramatic activity as the extremes of the other axis. At any point along this continuum, for example, dramatic activity can be more or less spontaneous and more or less teacher initiated:

Spontaneous

.

...

....

....

....

Child-initiated .... Teacher-initiated

....

....

....

...

.

Structured

15

One might argue that themes for drama, and perhaps for the entire curriculum, should evolve spontaneously from the children's interests. But this is not always practical, especially in structured settings, such as a kindergarten classroom, with an established curriculum and limited flexibility. There are also situations in which children's life experiences are limited, and it is desirable to engage them in dramatic activity that can broaden their exposure. For example, "A Trip to the Beach" was developed for children with little or no experience of the ocean.

Finally, ten or twenty children in a class will not all be on the same wavelength. Unless the setting provides for many opportunities to work in small groups, the teacher may be obliged to develop whole-group "circle-time" activities that accommodate the varying interests and abilities of the group. Flexibility and adaptability are key here. The continuum is thus intended to present the range of possibilities for dramatic activity and does not assign a value on one approach over the other.[1]

Using this continuum to identify methodology of process-oriented drama, three general patterns emerge: incidental drama, evolving drama, and preplanned drama.

INCIDENTAL DRAMA

This type of drama work evolves from the children's own dramatic play. The teacher integrates dramatic elements as a spontaneous response to and in conjunction with the unfolding play. This sometimes occurs naturally in classrooms or day-care settings where children have ample opportunity for dramatic play. It generally begins with observation, the teacher seeking an opportunity to expand the play by introducing a new character, prop, action, or conflict into the preexisting child-made drama. In "Superhero Alert," the teacher introduces a challenge to children acting out superhero scenarios of shooting and killing to come up with alternative solutions. The scenario of the children's unfolding dramatic play broadens in response to the "minidrama" introduced by the teacher. This kind of drama work often involves a small group of children and generally lasts between five and twenty minutes.[2]

EVOLVING DRAMA

Here again, the motivation for creating a drama experience comes from the children's play and expressed interest. For example, the story drama *The Very Busy Spider* (Chapter 7) was developed in response to children's fascination with a large web in the corner of the playroom. Once a clear direction in the children's play has been recognized, the teacher creates an introductory drama experience outside of the play setting to explore the theme or themes that have emerged. The structure of the ongoing drama work evolves from the children's response to and involvement in this initial drama work. Drama of this nature can take place in one session or continue for several days.

PREPLANNED DRAMA

The theme for a preplanned drama is usually predetermined by the curriculum, season, or a special event. "Your Own Back Yard," in Chapter 3, was developed to support a unit on recycling. Even though the teacher has planned the structure and overall direction of the drama, there remains a certain amount of flexibility and room for spontaneity. Drama of this nature can take place in one session but generally continues for several days (extended drama).

To stimulate children's curiosity about a subject, the preplanned drama can be initiated by establishing a related environment in the dramatic play area of the classroom. For example, the cardboard box village in "The Stranger" stayed up in the classroom for several days for the children to interact with outside of the more structured extended drama.

Planning Drama

A seasoned teacher relies more so on her own intuition than on a step-by-step lesson plan. It is the same with drama. With experience and confidence, teachers will respond to the unfolding interests of the children. Responsiveness and spontaneity keep the work fresh and child centered. This is particularly true when working with young children. As described earlier, the most child-centered drama work begins with children's expressed interests and takes its direction solely from the cues they offer.

However, using drama in a totally child-centered way requires experience and some familiarity with the medium. For this reason, it may be necessary for the beginning drama teacher to work more closely from a plan. The following step-by-step guide to developing a drama session or an extended drama is intended to provide this starting point. Over time and with practice, you will be able to create a drama plan that is skeletal, allowing the "fleshing out" to be determined by the children's enthusiasm as well as their verbal and nonverbal contributions.

The following guide to structuring drama delineates how to integrate a process-oriented approach into story dramatization (Chapters 2, 5, 6, and 7) or theme-based drama work (Chapters 3, 6, and 7). Each step is carefully laid out. Next, different approaches are outlined, and criteria are developed to help determine which approach is most suitable for a particular situation. This process is described in the context of specific examples of drama work presented throughout the text. Those that prefer to look at some concrete examples first should review Chapter 2 before continuing.

DETERMINING OBJECTIVES

There are three types of objectives to consider when planning a drama session or extended drama work: (1) the short- or long-term objectives of a given curriculum unit (such as colors or the seasons), (2) objectives related to specific aspects of child development (such as refining fine motor skills or developing self-control), and (3) those objectives intrinsic to drama (such as developing the imagination and creative self-expression). Keep in mind that in more spontaneous and child-initiated drama work, the objectives often evolve from the children's own choices.

Curricular Objectives We are using the term *curriculum* to refer to units or themes established not only for school or day-care settings, but also in church, arts, or recreational programs. This could be as elementary as "identifying and expressing the opposite of heavy and light" (see "Heavy Elephants and Light Butterflies," Chapter 7). But even a child as young as three can be engaged in much more sophisticated levels of thinking, such as "creating strategies to resolve fear and anger" (see *Kwa Doma Doma*, Chapter 6). In all these settings, drama can be used successfully to broaden the child's awareness and understanding of issues, themes, conflict, and types of people.

In story dramatization, one common objective is "to broaden the students' comprehension of the story's theme." Or perhaps the story itself is selected because it relates to a broader topic being covered in the curriculum. For example, if the curricular unit is "African Customs," and the teacher is using a *Zomo the Rabbit* story, the objective of the drama might be to reinforce the child's understanding of West African culture and not necessarily the trickster theme within the story. Related objectives might be: "to create the atmosphere of a West African village" or "to explore the tradition of storytelling in West Africa."

Developmental Objectives In addition to reinforcing the theme of a story, or related curricular topics, there are several developmental objectives that can be addressed through drama. The primary developmental goals for early childhood education are emotional, physical, social, linguistic, and cognitive development. Skills within these five broader categories include

- emotional skills such as identifying emotions, verbalizing feelings, conflict resolution, and a sense of self worth
- physical competencies such as sensory integration and gross and fine motor control
- social skills such as group cooperation, turn taking, self-expression, and sharing
- linguistic development, including increased vocabulary, use of language, dialogue, and negotiation
- cognitive development, including mastering conceptual skills, problem solving, numerology, and emerging literacy (Bredekamp 1997)

Most of the drama work within the text was developed to broaden the children's awareness and understanding of specific issues and themes. However, developmental aims also were considered and intentionally incorporated into much of this work. Additionally, some of the drama work reported within the text was designed specifically to support child development in a certain area (see Chapter 6).

Though the drama can be specifically structured to foster developmental growth, much of this development occurs naturally as a holistic outgrowth of the drama work. The natural, intrinsic value of drama is examined next.

Intrinsic Objectives There are many benefits that are intrinsic to process-oriented drama for children. These include creative expression (physical and verbal), inter- and intrapersonal development (social and self-awareness), practice in language use (physical and verbal), and the development of the imagination (Gardner 1990).

The intrinsic value of drama alone provides a valid argument for using drama with young children. Indeed there are those in the field that strongly believe in "art for art's sake." Some schools do allow time for all four of the arts in this way. When this is not the case, however, drama can support both intrinsic and more formal instructional objectives.

When determining appropriate objectives for a drama, it is helpful to consider the following questions:

- What is the current theme being addressed in the curriculum?
- What topics or skills (developmentally, or otherwise) are currently being covered in other areas of the curriculum that might cross over to this drama?
- What other types of development could be reinforced within the context of the drama?
- What intrinsic benefits could be emphasized in this session?

· ·

CREATING A SCENARIO AND DETERMINING CHARACTERS

Once the objectives of the drama are established, a scenario can be developed that will serve as a framework.

Story Dramatization Children's literature is often the easiest dramatic material for beginners, as the story provides a ready-made plot. The plot may be simplified and some characters excluded from the dramatization, but the sequence of events (sometimes the most challenging aspect of structuring drama) is already established.

The role(s) children portray in the story will be based on which character perspective would be most valuable for them to experience. For this purpose, you may also wish to have them change roles or switch back and forth between two important characters. For example, in the story dramatization of *Where the Wild Things Are,* by Maurice Sendack, all the children initially portray the character of Max until Max encounters the Wild Things; at this point, children switch roles and become Wild Things. This allows them to experience the freedom and wildness personified by these imaginary characters. As the drama ends, children return to the role of Max and share the feeling of returning safely home to love and acceptance.

Whether or not you dramatize the entire story depends on how much time is available, and how relevant it might be for the children to experience the entire sequence of the story. It is possible that you may want to only dramatize a small segment. This works nicely to emphasize a particular point or simply to spark the children's interest in the literature. Directions for creating each scene or step of the scenario are explained later, in "Separating the Drama into Scenes."

Theme-based Drama When drama is used to explore a theme, your objectives will help you develop a dramatic scenario. For example, "Caring for the Environment" is a common theme that is introduced to children as young as preschool. Most frequently the classroom work revolves around recycling. In the drama "Your Own Back Yard," recycling is only one aspect of the work. The scenario evolved from what the children had already been studying, their neighborhood and the animals they were familiar with (birds, squirrels, and cats). The primary objective is "to demonstrate an awareness of the effect pollution has on the environment and employ related problem-solving strategies." The teacher developed two problems for the children to encounter: people in a crowded neighborhood dumping trash and garbage in the park, and air pollution caused by too many cars in the neighborhood. The children, in the role of the animals suffering the effects of the pollution, become the protagonists of the scenario (birds and squirrels that live in the park). The teacher facilitated the "problem-solving" aspect of the objective by taking on the role of an alley cat, who encourages the birds and squirrels to develop a plan that will help the humans realize what damage their pollution is causing.

In "Space Travel" (Chapter 3), the theme-related objective is "to broaden the children's curiosity and awareness of the sun, moon, and stars" and "to become aware of distance." The drama involves children in the role of space pioneers who travel by rocket to the moon. The scenario is a journey into outerspace, including preparation, travel, a visit to the moon, returning home, and celebration, with the parents (in role as reporters) engaging the space pioneers in recall. "The Hospital" (Chapter 3) was developed to demystify medical settings, procedures, and roles, and to let the children take charge of a potentially disempowering situation. A hospital environment is created and the scenario evolves as children and teacher construct a hospital in the classroom and take turns trying out all the roles, from patient to anesthetist.

SEQUENCING EVENTS

Though the majority of the drama sessions and extended dramas described in this book might appear to have a sequential order of events, it isn't necessary nor always suitable to follow a linear format. Child-initiated work will often progress in a seemingly illogical direction. Unless there is a "silly" aspect to the direction of their work, this can be a valuable and holistic way of working. In a follow-up to the dramatization of *Where the Wild Things Are,* one child took Max's boat across the ocean to find a circus. While you don't need to cross the Pacific to find clowns, this progression made emotional sense for that particular child.

You may also find it useful to move the drama backwards in time (though this is difficult for some three- and early four-year-old children to grasp). In "Your Own Back Yard," children go back into the past to discover how clean and beautiful the park had been before it became polluted. In "The Stranger" (Chapter 3), they are able to peek into the window of Emma's past and view her life before she became homeless. This technique also can be used in story drama, allowing the children to consider events that led up to the situation in the story. In *Brave Irene* (Chapter 2), children can more fully understand the value of the dress Irene's mother makes for the Duchess by taking time to design and create dresses before the story begins. Imagining or recalling the past helps children make connections and consider consequences.

ESTABLISHING AN APPROPRIATE INTRODUCTION

Drama work is often preceded by related classroom work, whether or not it is intended as preparation for the drama or simply part of the related unit. No matter how much related background information children have covered, it is still essential to establish a clear and purposeful beginning and ending to each drama session. The introduction has three main purposes:

1. to establish the beginning of "drama time," helping children transition from their previous work
2. to introduce the characters and setting in the imaginary world of the drama
3. to introduce and reinforce new vocabulary and concepts.

Time for Drama Transitions from one activity to the next are difficult for young children. Transitioning into the drama (and back out) is particularly important. There are generally different rules of behavior for drama, such as more freedom of movement, more noise allowed, and different use of the space and furniture. It is helpful to establish a regular space where drama begins and perhaps a ritual or routine activity that establishes the special qualities of drama.

Initially, for children new to drama, the teacher might begin each session by reviewing what drama time means: "Remember, in drama we use our imaginations. Just like play time, we can pretend to be somebody else and we can pretend to be in some other place. We can even pretend that it is nighttime when it is really day, or winter when it is really summer. Pretending is using our imaginations."

Some teachers begin each drama session with a simple routine or ritual, such as "dusting" the heads of the children with an "imagination duster," sprinkling some "magic sparkles" into the air, or having children mime putting on their imaginary "drama shoes." The imaginary shoes can be used to transform children into a character or magically transport them anywhere they want to go. Beginning drama with this type of ritual is particularly effective for young children, as they take comfort in the familiarity of repetition.

Other ways of using a ritual to initiate the beginning of drama time include

Using a whirligig to "fly" to an imaginary place, as suggested for *Giant Jam Sandwich* (Chapter 2)
Passing a large sea shell around for children to "hear the story" in *Sky Woman* (Chapter 5)

The ritualized use of sage in *Sky Woman* and *The Mud Pony* (Chapter 2), derived from Native American tradition

Creating Imaginary Characters and Setting More relevant to the specific drama work is an introduction or ritual that will help children enter the imaginary world of the drama. This world will consist of new characters and setting, and there are several means for introducing them to the children.

In *Kwa Doma Doma* (Chapter 6), the introduction involves a multisensory airplane journey to South Africa. Then children create their characters and establish the environment of South African villagers. First they experience the sun, then sitting by an imaginary river, they listen to South African music and sound effects. Next they make earrings, rings, bracelets, headbands, foot bracelets, and so on, from tapestry loops. Now they are ready to listen to the story.

Before taking on a character in the main part of the drama, the children might practice or explore defining qualities and characteristics. In *Lance the Giraffe* (Chapter 2), children all become giraffes, putting on their imaginary spots and stretching tall necks to eat the leaves off of trees.

Other introductory work that establishes character and/or setting include

Having the children physicalize the environment, such as becoming the stones that form a Greek Island in *Persephone* (Chapter 5)
Building an environment from a single sensory cue, such as listening to the sea inside a shell ("A Trip to the Beach," Chapter 3)
Pointing out the distinguishing gifts of a specific culture, such as the Seven Nations' peoples' ability to interpret the language of nature (*Sky Woman,* Chapter 5)
Choosing mask, costume pieces, and props to explore animal and people characteristics (*Bread and Honey*, Chapter 2)

New Vocabulary and Concepts If there has been little or no pretext to the drama work, it may be necessary to introduce new vocabulary and concepts essential to understanding the drama. Before dramatizing *Persephone,* for example, adequate time should be alotted to introduce the seasons, depending on how much the children already know and what other work they are currently doing in relation to this topic.

Creative movement is a good medium for exploring new concepts. In "Heavy Elephants and Light Butterflies," these opposites are explored by imitating the movement of falling tissue and feathers. Then, in contrast, children stomp their feet in imitation of a "heavy" block being dropped. In the introduction to "Preparing for Winter," children explore the concept of hibernation by becoming bears, spending a good amount of time exploring "bear movement." Techniques that may be new to children, such as miming, moving in slow motion, or freezing should also be introduced and "practiced." In *Persephone*, children practice "freezing" and "melting."

Other ways of introducing new vocabulary, concepts, and techniques within the introduction include

> Experiencing smells, tastes, and colors of autumn in preparation for "Autumn Leaves," (Chapter 7)
>
> Creating a dream space to explore the difference between dreams and reality in *The Mud Pony* (Chapter 2)
>
> Practicing a technique to be used, such as "mirroring" before becoming the monkeys in *Caps for Sale* (Chapter 2)

ESTABLISHING AN APPROPRIATE CLOSING

Closure is a vital element of the drama session. It helps create a solid boundary around the event and enables children to return to the world of their classroom and not remain "stuck" in the story. In addition to helping children leave the imaginary world of the drama, the closing should provide an opportunity to reflect on what has just transpired and, if necessary, to process it. The opening (introduction) and closing of the drama serve as bookends, separating the fantasy of the drama from the reality of the classroom.

Leaving the Imaginary World Returning to reality is an important transition. Not only must children be made aware that their "pretend play" has ended, they must also let go of any high energy stimulated by the drama work. The closing should be soothing and calming. Generally, an activity that ends with children seated in the circle or even lying on the floor works well. Many of the reported dramas in this book end with the children, "in character," pretending to fall asleep and waking up as themselves again "back in the classroom."

In the (five-day) story dramatization of *The Mud Pony,* each child takes on the role of a Pawnee Indian child whose pretend mud pony becomes real. At the end of the first day's dramatization of a buffalo hunt, the children pretend to sleep around the embers of the campfire. Each child is wrapped in the blanket they use at school for nap. The blanket becomes the transitional object that transforms the children from the boy in the drama back to the security of the classroom and their real-life identities.

Other ways of leaving the imaginary world of the drama include

> Transforming the body of the character back into the body of a child, for example, using feathers to gently tickle a bird back into a child (*Sky Woman,* Chapter 6)

Shrinking a big image (spider) to a small one (stick-on spider star) (*The Very Busy Spider,* Chapter 7)
Clearing away props that made the environment (for example, the "village" boxes) ("The Stranger," Chapter 3)

Processing the Drama The closing also allows children to begin synthesizing the drama work. If the drama session has been unusually stimulating, an art activity as simple as making a picture of what the children remember from the experience can be quite effective. Art or some type of story-recall task allows children "to "ex-press," to draw out any images that might otherwise distract them from focusing on the next part of their day. After a session in which the children have become birds (*Sky Woman*) and experienced the thrill of "flying through the air," the teacher gives them construction paper and chalk to illustrate their flight. Focusing on the art project and listening to soothing music enable children to process and gain control of any charged emotions that might otherwise lead to agitation in class.

Other ways of using the closing to begin processing the drama work include

Making maps in *The Mud Pony* (Chapter 2); helps children conceptualize the journey they've just taken in the drama
Verbalizing their personal feelings, such as children sharing their experiences of "getting in trouble" after dramatizing *Where the Wild Things Are* (Chapter 6)

SEPARATING THE DRAMA INTO SCENES

Once the introduction is established, the scenario of the drama can unfold. Initially, teachers may want the drama session to be quite structured, in which case it is helpful to determine the sequence of events ahead of time. This kind of preparation is particularly helpful for those starting out, but eventually the overall structure should be flexible and allow for new developments initiated by the children.

The method proposed here for structuring a drama scenario is similar to a technique used by many theatre directors. It requires breaking the scenario down into "beats," or short scenes. (In theatre they are referred to as "French scenes." Before rehearsals start, the script is broken down into short scenes that indicate the entrance of a new character or a change in place or time.) Although a drama teacher, unlike a director, is not preparing for a final production, this method works quite well in setting out the sequence of a story drama or theme-based drama. Similar to script work, the two best indicators for determining a "scene break" are

- a major change of place or time
- the appearance of a new character

At each of these scene breaks, the teacher can stop to regroup, preparing the children for the new setting or taking time to change roles.

Story Dramatization The scenes of a story are already established. It is usually quite simple to break the story into short scenes by identifying the change of time or place and the entrance of new characters. Some stories may need to be streamlined to eliminate any scenes that complicate the work or simply to cut back on time.

The dramatization of *Where the Wild Things Are* is broken down into eight scenes: (1) Max making mischief, (2) Max's mother arriving on the scene, (3) Max in his room, (4) the journey across the sea, (5) Max's arrival to the place of the Wild Things, (6) the Wild Things "making rumpus," (7) the return trip, and (8) back home. At each point, the teacher gathers the children together for a minidiscussion of what transpired and/or preparation for the next scene.

Theme-based Drama When the drama is based on a specific theme, the teacher creates the storyline from scratch. The scenario can initially be done as a very loose outline, adding scenes and filling out the details as the work progresses. The number of scenes is often dependent on the amount of time allowed for the drama work, though it is nice to have some flexibility to extend the drama if children are enthusiastically engaged.

There are various ways to organize scene breaks. For example, each new scene in the drama work might begin with children moving back into a circle or a set meeting place to introduce the next scene. Frequent breaks in the work are necessary to regroup and may need to occur as often as every five or ten minutes, especially for threes and early fours. The important thing is that the scene breaks make sense to you.

In the theme-based drama "The Stranger," the children first spend three days creating their village and constitution, then Emma—a homeless woman—visits the village at night while the villagers are "asleep" in their houses. Emma's departure signals a natural scene break. In the next scene it is morning and "the villagers" assemble in "the village square" (seated around a table) to discuss the events of the previous night. The decision to build Emma a home of her own transitions spontaneously into the next scene, in which the villagers disperse to gather "building materials and furniture" for the house. In the final scene, the villagers go home to their beds to await Emma's return.

Determining the Best Approach

Once the scenario or sequence of scenes has been organized, the next step is to determine what approach to take for each scene. Should everyone become baby bats gliding through the air and hanging upside down, or should they use their hands to represent bat wings and portray Stellaluna's first flight (*Stellaluna*)? Will one large spaceship be created for all to climb into, or will they stay seated in their own imaginary spaceships ("Space Travel")? Should they, as Wild Things, make rumpus within the safety of the circle, or should they be allowed to use the whole room to create a feeling of freedom? To sustain interest and involvement, it is best to change the approach from scene to scene. Possible variations include

- introducing new types of dramatic activity
- changing the way children are grouped
- intensifying or decreasing the level of participation
- using a different space
- switching or changing roles

There are several ways to categorize drama methodology and technique. What we've attempted to do is identify strategies that are best suited to young children and that are most frequently represented in this book. The following discussion explores three primary considerations when looking for the best approach: type of dramatic activity, grouping, and level of physical activity.

TYPES OF DRAMATIC ACTIVITY

For each scene or phase of the drama work, a specific type of dramatic activity must be identified that will best facilitate meaningful involvement for each child. Indeed, just as you have established an overall objective for the work, each scene, or phase of the drama, will have a specific aim. Determining what approach to take with each scene will generally be based on the specific experience you wish to create or what character perspective you would like the children to explore. The story drama of *The Mud Pony* is designed to enhance creative problem-solving strategies. The Pawnee boy in the story faces a series of overwhelming problems. Each time, the solution comes from inside himself, until finally a miracle does occur.

Once you've determined the purpose, as well as the needs and abilities of the children at that particular point in the work, planning your approach to the scene will be fairly logical. In *The Mud Pony,* the boy's material deprivation—his "hunger"—is twofold: He lacks both food and possessions, specifically the beautiful ponies that all the other children have. The teacher wanted the children to experience how the boy satisfied this hunger by creating his own pony out of the scanty resources available to him: mud and imagination. The children all take on the role of the boy, making "mud ponies" out of finger paint. Only, what looks like plain old finger paint is really chocolate pudding. Half way through the project, they realize that their art project is in fact delicious food.

Even if you are using a linear sequence, it is not necessary for children to stay in role, dramatizing the action of the scenario in each scene. Extending one particular role or ongoing action for too long is too demanding (if not impossible) for young children, and they will quickly lose focus. The best way to maintain young children's participation is by changing the type of dramatic activity for each step or scene within a session.

Most of the dramatic activity found in this book requires that the children be engaged in the characters, setting, or dramatic action. (Dramatic activities such as playmaking, theatre games, and "getting to know you" activities are not included.) Most drama of this nature would fall under these categories: creative movement, puppetry and hand-play, miming the action, and improvisation.

Creative Movement Movement is a wonderful way for children to express and explore feelings and ideas. Not only is it well suited to the young child's most natural means of communicating (through gesture and movement), the latest brain research presents strong evidence that movement (lots of it) plays an essential role in thinking and learning as well as the crucial development of sensory integration. A young child is most likely to recall a new word, concept, or sequence of information when movement has been part of the learning experience.[3]

Within the context of a drama session, creative movement can be used to explore emotion, animal movement, and environment, such as growing plants, rain, wind, ocean waves, falling leaves, and swaying trees. Children kinesthetically absorb concepts within these categories such as weight, speed, size, shape, and opposites.[4]

Other examples of creative movement include the following:

Exploring terrains and their wildlife, such as becoming birds, fish, and pieces of the sky in *Sky Woman*
Experiencing contrasts in movement, as children do in "Your Own Back Yard," becoming squirrels and birds
Personifying aspects of weather, such as the wind in *Mirandy and Brother Wind* (Chapter 2), *Persephone,* and *Brave Irene*

Puppetry and Hand-Play In the early stages of dramatic play, children begin to use props, toys, and dolls as symbols for their thoughts, feelings, and needs. Teachers as well as therapists of young children know that children resistant to communication will often express their feelings and ideas through a puppet. The puppet need not be sophisticated or authentic in nature. Even a wooden spoon with eyes attached will serve this purpose. In several of the drama sessions in this text, children use their hands as the puppet. Even objects from the drama, such as trees, boats, and rain, are represented by the children's hands. This allows children to explore the dramatic action on a symbolic level (prereading) and provides for kinesthetic learning.

Working this way is particularly effective for drawing out language from troubled or extremely introverted children. The puppets, props, and hand shapes also facilitate comprehension and development of language for language-delayed children and children learning a second language (see Chapter 7).

Most children are fascinated with this miniature form of theatre, making the use of puppets and hand-play an excellent tool for maintaining focus and enthusiasm. It also provides a means for keeping children involved while they are seated and focused.[5]

Other examples (all from Chapter 2) of puppetry and hand-play include

Use of hands and arms to create giraffes, other animals, and environment in the story drama *Lance the Giraffe,* moving back and forth throughout the drama from hand-play to whole-body action
Simple prop puppets, such as clothespins becoming wasps in *The Giant Jam Sandwich*
Simple glove puppets, created using black gloves to make spiders in *The Very Busy Spider* and surgical gloves as bats in *Stellaluna*

Miming the Action A great deal of drama work involves miming the action of the scene. Props and scenery for every action are simply not necessary in this type of work, not only because of the impracticality of creating and managing a number of props with children. Miming the action encourages use of imagination and spontaneity. When a group of children uses mime to act out carrying a baby animal, climbing a tree, or flying over the ocean, each child's vision of that experience is unique.

One common technique used to keep children involved, while maintaining control, is to have them mime the action of the drama while seated or standing. The potentially wild action of "blasting off" in "Space Travel" is all done in place, with children leaning back against upside down chairs. They travel thousands of miles without moving from their

spots. Though the drama work for *The Mud Pony* involves children galloping about the room, this could also be done sitting in a circle, clopping
fists on the ground to represent galloping.

When props *are* used in the work described in this book, they are
symbolic in nature, furthering children's imaginations and thinking (see
the section on props in Chapter 4). Miming the action of the drama should
not be overused, as it can somewhat limit the experience. It is useful, however, in varying the children's involvement, especially for children who
may become overstimulated or confused by free-range movement.

More examples of drama work that use mime include the following:

As a whole group, children mime pulling up the sky tree in *Sky
Woman* (Chapter 5).
The teacher, as Demeter, directs the "hungry people" to mime lift-
ing the ice mountain in *Persephone* (Chapter 5).
Individually, children create mimed mischief as well as the boat trip
in *Where the Wild Things Are* (Chapter 2).

Improvisation In the context of process drama for young children, improvisation is the primary mode of dramatic activity. Even the previously described creative movement and mime work are largely improvisational in
nature. Improvisation is used across the continuum of dramatic activity
to develop dialogue and action, including activity in highly structured
drama episodes. In addition to developing the plot or progression of the
drama, improvisation is frequently used as the medium for problem solving. In "A Trip to the Beach," children must devise and show through improvisation their escape from the belly of the whale.

Pure improvisational drama work is highly spontaneous, with little
guidance from the teacher other than the initial description of the
character(s) or situation to be improvised. When working with three- and
early four-year-old children, however, it might be necessary to verbally
guide children through the improvisation, using questions to draw out
their ideas.

Examples of dramatic activity that is purely improvisational include
the following:

Children improvise becoming medical personnel and patients in
"The Hospital," and the various roles and situations inspired by
"The Restaurant" theme drama (Chapter 3).
Children become leaves and take an imaginary journey, entirely
improvised, in "Leaf Journey" (Chapter 7).

GROUPING

Another consideration when planning a specific scene is how the children will be grouped to best facilitate the learning experience. Should they work individually, in pairs, in small groups, or as one large group? Again, this will depend on what perspective you want the children to experience as well as the situation of the scene.

Whole Group A great deal of the drama work in this book takes place with children working together as one large group. This is usually the easiest grouping to lead, as all are working simultaneously, taking their cues from the teacher.

Examples of large group work include

Participating in a cooperative group project, such as a tribal buffalo hunt in *The Mud Pony* and creating a village in "The Stranger"
Learning the power of community in *Kwa Doma Doma* (Chapter 6), when the group of villagers must work together to escape the monster's belly

Individual Work With story drama in particular, it is best if all the children can portray the protagonist of the story. This can still be done as a group activity. The children are each acting individually, as if they were the one and only character from the story or theme-based scenario. This works quite well with young children, who rarely question why there are twenty of the same character, each performing the same task at the same time. Even when this requires young children to play a character of a different gender, there is usually complete acceptance.

Most of the dramatizations in this text incorporate simultaneous role play. Drama work wherein this approach is primarily used includes

All children taking on the role of Irene (*Brave Irene*)
The role of Max (*Where the Wild Things Are*)
The role of "the lost boy" (*The Mud Pony*)
The role of Lance (*Lance the Giraffe*)
All experiencing the little bunny's bedtime routine in *Good Night Moon* (Chapter 7)

Working in Pairs Placing children in pairs (usually two characters talking or working together) is an excellent means of encouraging language development and providing opportunity for dialogue. This type of grouping works particularly well when there are two primary characters in the story. Several of the drama sessions in the text end with children seated with a partner, recalling the events, or sharing feelings about the drama in role, such as in *Bread and Honey*, when pairs of children (one as Ben and one as a parent) recall the trip home. Ben tells his parent about all the animals he met, with the child in the parent role asking questions.

When there are several partners working at the same time, the noise level can be quite high, which can be a problem in some classroom settings. However, it is well worth the trouble, as this is such an excellent opportunity for practicing communication skills and children usually stay on task. The teacher, and any adult assistants, should travel among the pairs, facilitating the conversation of those getting stuck, confused, or way off track. It is also helpful to pair a strong communicator with a less verbal child.

Other uses of pair work within the drama session are

> Cooperative tasks, such as the butterfly and elephant partners problem solving in "Heavy Elephants and Light Butterflies" (Chapter 7)
> Practicing communication skills, such as Irene describing her adventures to her mother in *Brave Irene*

Small Groups In some situations, it may be necessary to create small groups (three to five children per group) that are working simultaneously in different areas of the room. This approach works nicely for creative work and cooperative problem solving. There are several children's books in which one character travels around to meet or discuss a problem with other individual characters. *Bread and Honey* (Chapter 2) and *Are You My Mother?* (Chapter 7) are good examples. Instead of selecting one child per character, divide the whole class into character groupings. In the story dramatization of *Bread and Honey*, for example, instead of visiting the owl, bunny, lion, and so on, Ben stops to visit a *group* of owls, bunnies, and lions. You may need to reduce the number of story characters to no more than six. This is the most challenging drama grouping for very young children (perhaps too difficult for early threes and children with special needs) and usually requires more than one adult to facilitate the work. For three-year-olds, reduce the number to two to three groupings per adult.

Other uses of children working together in small groups include

> Establishing different "work" areas, as in "The Hospital"
> and "The Restaurant" (Chapter 3)
> Practicing decision making and working cooperatively, as when
> groups of three or four children set up shops or houses in *Caps for Sale* (Chapter 2)

PHYSICAL ACTIVITY AND SPACE

Activity Level Varying the level of activity every few minutes is essential when working with young children. Although you want them to be participating as much of the time as is possible, this cannot be maintained at a high activity level. The drama sessions and extended dramas in this book demonstrate several levels of activity, including

- moving freely around the room
- moving within "the circle"
- moving in place: standing or seated
- lying down

Consider the energetic level of the prior scene and decide whether the next scene should be at a higher or lower level. If the children have just been "wasps" flying around the room, the following scene might best be played sitting in a circle (using hands to represent the wasps' action) or even lying down (wasps napping). In *The Mud Pony,* after becoming wild ponies prancing across the plains, children are summoned back into the circle. In the circle, the "ponies," hungry from their long journey, stop for oats (granola) and water. Children then lie down for naps and are wrapped in the pony's warm blanket. Children can be active participants on any level: seated, moving in place, moving around the circle, or free to move anywhere that's been designated as drama space.

Teachers who either are new to drama or are working with three-year-olds or children with special needs may feel more comfortable keeping as much of the movement as possible in the circle, preferably seated. Children are still able to participate in the action of the story through mime. As discussed earlier, they could also use props, puppets, or even hand-play, to present the action on a miniature scale. This integrates fine motor skills with the gross motor activity. When dramatizing the story *The Very Hungry Caterpillar* (Chapter 7), children start out using their finger to represent the caterpillar (with a pipe cleaner wrapped around each child's index finger to create antennas). As the drama progresses, children become caterpillars, crawling freely about the room. Butterflies are also represented with hands by creating wings. Later, children use their whole bodies to represent the butterfly, flying around the room to gentle music.

Space Many of the drama sessions and extended dramas in this book involve the expansion and contraction of space. Often a story drama will open with a single image—a color, an animal, a season—which is then incorporated into a story circle, expanded into a full classroom dramatic activity, and finally contracted and made more interior again during the closing. Some drama sessions alternate between dramatizing the events through the miniature scale of sign language and acting it out in full scale (*Lance the Giraffe, Where the Wild Things Are, The Very Hungry Caterpillar*).

The logic behind this variation is aesthetic, certainly, but also cognitive. One of the foundations of mathematical thinking is amplification and reduction, things getting bigger and things getting smaller. It's the first concept introduced in the greatest mathematical allegory of all time, *Alice in Wonderland*. First Alice grows huge, then she becomes small.

In *The Very Busy Spider,* children are asked to imagine a spider the size of their hands, then the size of their whole bodies, as big as the whole room, and finally, the size of a tiny star sticker. Yet this cognitive challenge is no greater than the one that asks them to look at a number that, like the spider, is a constant but keeps expanding and contracting according to its context. Five grains of rice here, five buses there.

Ideally, children should be up on their feet, "living through" the drama at key points within the session, when possible. Though difficult to maintain for any length of time, you can alternate this with calming activity by frequently stopping to regroup. Whatever level of physical activity and use of space you choose, keeping this varied will keep the children interested, without losing focus.

Transitioning Between the Scenes

Stopping to regroup and change the level of activity also allows you to prepare the children for a new setting or change in role. These transitions between scenes are an important refocusing time for young children. The transition should redirect the energy of the group, for example, adding a soothing chant while moving from a high-energy, expressive activity to something quieter and more reflective, or vice versa. Not only does this keep children's energy level in balance, and therefore under control, it is also more artful, more aesthetic.

Sometimes the teacher's voice narrating the beginning of a new scene is sufficient. In *Where the Wild Things Are,* the teacher softly narrates from Sendak's book, "Max sailed back home, over a year and in and out of weeks and through a day and into the night of his very own room." Then she adds, "Do you know what Max found in his very own room? His supper, and it was still warm. Max, take off your wolf costume." (Children mime taking it off while seated.) The children, previously in character as Wild Things, have made the transition back into the role of Max, back in his room eating his supper.

It may also be necessary to regroup with a "planning meeting" between the scenes. This can be a brief discussion about what just occurred and/or what is coming up next. When the sequence of the drama is child initiated, the transition time can be used to explore where the drama will lead, through questioning. The villagers in "The Stranger" meet a few times for the purpose of problem solving. The decisions they make determine the direction of the next scene.

If children are changing characters or setting, some time needs to be taken to prepare, mentally and physically, for this transition. Sometimes a prop, a noisemaker such as a wind tube or a chime, or even a tactile stimulus may be necessary to interrupt an exciting high-stimulus scene and facilitate a change of role or place. When the "wasps" reach fever pitch, introduce a sudden shower of rain and instruct them to return to the shelter of their wasp nests. The rain washes off their "wasp features" and turns them back into "villagers." In *Sky Woman,* after becoming birds catching the falling light, children change roles by using a feather to brush off their bird features, ready to become a new character in the story. (See Chapter 4 for more information on using props to facilitate scene transitions.)

Suitable Roles for Children and Teacher

ROLES FOR CHILDREN

Several of the drama episodes in this text engage children in more than one role during a drama session. Sometimes they are moving back and forth between roles, or in and out of roles every few minutes. Often all are playing the same role simultaneously. Their ability to do so with relative ease is a unique characteristic of this age group (see Introduction).

Generally, it is best to allow all of the children to become the protagonist in the story. This is the case in many of the story dramas presented in the book. They are simultaneously experiencing Max's frustration in *Where the Wild Things Are,* Mirandy's joy when she captures the wind (*Mirandy and Brother Wind*), and the abandoned Pawnee child's awe when his mud pony becomes real (*The Mud Pony*). Some scenarios involve an important interaction between two primary characters. It is possible to have children switch between roles, as in *Stellaluna,* when children portray the baby bat and baby birds. If you decide to divide children into pairs (such as Irene and her mother in *Brave Irene*), allow time for them to switch roles and experience both perspectives. Archetypal roles, such as Sky Woman and Kwa Doma Doma are not appropriate for children at this age.

Exceptions to playing specific roles are when the story or scenario requires a group effort, such as the villager's determining the fate of the homeless stranger in "The Stranger," or astronauts journeying through space in "Space Travel." When they are in role as members of a group, they experience being part of a community and discovering the value of working together to solve a problem.

ROLES FOR TEACHERS

Finally, you need to decide on the level of teacher involvement in each scene. Should you play a character and direct the action, or coach from the sidelines? Try to vary this as well. Preschool and kindergarten children respond very well when the teacher becomes involved in the drama as another character. The teacher's involvement also serves as a role model for the children, modeling her commitment to the drama. Leading the drama in role is also an excellent technique for engaging children in dialogue.

Acting skills are not a prerequisite, as young children need very little convincing to believe the character is genuine. A simple prop, such as a hat, scarf, or apron, or even a slight change in voice or stature is enough to convince and engage children. Remove the prop to move back and forth between character(s) and the teacher role, giving instructions about the action or dialogue as needed. This can also be done if there is a need to return to a teacher role during the drama to take care of discipline issues or other business, before reverting once again to the character role. It is even possible to change roles, using a different prop for each character. Many of the dramatizations incorporate teaching-in-role, including the teacher in role as

Ben's mother in *Bread and Honey*
The homeless stranger in "The Stranger"
The alley cat in "Your Own Back Yard"

The teacher must make it clear to the children that she is only pretending to be the character and can return as the teacher by removing the prop: "When I put this hat on, I will be the capseller. Look, now I will take the hat off again. Who am I now?"

Certain character types may be too frightening for children to intereact with. One of the authors observed a Head Start teacher trying to lead a Halloween drama in the role of a witch. She carefully explained to the group of three-year-olds that when she had the witch's hat on she would be the witch and when she took it off she would be the teacher again, but every time she put the hat on and changed her voice, children screamed and cried. Taking the hat off calmed them instantly, but they never believed the witch was just the teacher pretending. One astute child later informed the teacher that "the witch had shoes just like yours." Scary characters can be softened by adding humor, as in *Persephone*, when Hades is portrayed as a clown-like fellow.

USING MASKS, MAKEUP, AND COSTUMES TO CREATE ROLE

Masks An important consideration in the preschool classroom is the way children understand mask. Earlier we discussed the fine line between reality and fantasy for a child in this age group. Most adults think of masks as disguises—false faces. Young children, however, easily interpret them as real. The way a child sees a mask is much closer to archaic tradition (and many contemporary non-Western cultures).[6] A mask replaces one identity with another; a new face creates a new person. By this logic, when a familiar, trusted teacher puts on a Halloween mask, she disappears from the room and her class is left in the thrall of a scary witch.

This does not mean that mask should be jettisoned from the curriculum, but rather used with respect for a child's reality. Examples of mask use to create a role include

Wearing paper plate masks as a "necklace," as children do to remind themselves to which animal group they belong, in *Bread and Honey*
The teacher using, but not necessarily wearing, a large mask to represent an archetypal character, such as the masks of Demeter and Persephone described in Chapter 5

Makeup and Costume With a dab of makeup or wearing a simple costume, a teacher can achieve sufficient identity change to "suspend disbelief" while still being identifiable as her everyday self. Costumes (and masks) that are too enveloping may take away the child's capacity to identify the real world component—the teacher under the mask or wig.

The teacher only wearing a scarf, as opposed to a full costume, when playing Max's mother works better. It matches children's rhythm of moving between fantasy and reality and reassures them that their real world is not altogether lost.

In *Sky Woman,* the dramatic character of Sky Woman is costumed not masked. The scene in which she falls from the sky is dramatic enough without the addition of a mask. A young child's capacity to move in and out of an imaginary world is such that, in one moment, they could be fully engaged with Sky Woman on the turtle's back, and in the next, checking out that she's really their teacher in a wig and funny-colored dress.

When it comes to costuming children, shifting into character takes very little stimulation. Getting on all fours with a black streak down their noses transforms a class of four-year-old children into a herd of ponies in *The Mud Pony.*

The following are other examples of makeup and costume being used to create a character:

> Makeup: Children paint giraffe spots on their faces to celebrate Lance's discovery in *Lance the Giraffe.*
> Small costume pieces: The teacher puts on an apron to portray Ben's mother baking in *Bread and Honey.*
> Large costume pieces: The teacher uses an old coat and makeup to become Emma in "The Stranger."

In summary, the following steps can be used to create a plan for drama:

- Determine your objectives: curricular, developmental, and intrinsic.
- Develop the scenario and characters to be dramatized.
- Create an introduction to the drama session that establishes time for drama, develops the imaginary characters and setting, and/or introduces new concepts and vocabulary.
- Break the scenario into steps or specific scenes that delineate new characters or a new setting.
- Create a closing to help children leave the imaginary world of the drama and process their work.

This will serve as a flexible outline that may change and evolve with the children's response and interest. Once this outline is established, there are several factors to consider to help you determine the best approach for each step or scene:

- Type of dramatic activity: creative movement, puppetry, and hand-play, pantomime, and improvisation
- Grouping: whole group, small groups, pairs, and individual work
- Physical activity and space: moving freely around the room; moving within "the circle"; moving in place; standing, seated, or lying down, use of small, regular, or large scale
- Suitable roles for children and teacher
- Transitions between the scenes to facilitate changes in role, setting, grouping, and level of activity.

Notes

1. Gavin Bolton provides an in-depth discussion of the nature of dramatic activity (referred to as classification of dramatic activity), in his book *Toward a Theory of Drama in Education*. 1979. Heinemann: Portsmouth, NH.

2. This approach is based on the notion of scaffolding—a familiar term in early childhood education, referencing supportive adult intervention in the play of young children (Vygotsky 1967; Smilansky and Shefatya 1990; Ford 1993).

3. For a thorough examination of the importance of movement in learning, we highly recommend Carla Hannaford's book *Smart Moves: Why Learning is Not All in Your Head*. 1995. Arlington, VA: Great Ocean Publishers.

4. A series of movement exercises (called Brain Gym) have been developed to facilitate concentration and enhance whole-brain movement. We recommend using these exercises which can be integrated into creative movement activity for young children and can effect immediate improvement in behavior and focus. See Dennison, P. E., and G. E. Dennison. *Brain Gym, Teacher's Edition*. 1989. Ventura, CA: Edu-Kinesthetics, Inc.

5. There are many excellent resources for learning more about the creation and use of puppetry with young children. Discussion and examples within this book are purposefully limited to keep the focus on drama. See Hunt, Tamara, and Nancy Renfro. *Puppetry in Early Childhood*. 1982. Austin, TX: Nancy Renfro Studios.

6. Stephen and Robin Larsen in "The Healing Mask," an essay in *Parabola*, (volume VI, number 3, Mask and Metaphor), write, "Modern attitudes to the mask have stressed its concealing role: The social mask one hides behind, the cosmetic mask with its painted expression, the sinister mask of the headsman. . . . But perhaps closer to the archaic meaning is that of a mask worn to carnival . . . a transformation of character takes place. . . . There is a glimpse of the inner cast of characters which inhabits each one of us."

2

Stepping into Stories

Children's literature and stories are an excellent resource for drama with young children. Storytime is a popular daily ritual in preschool and kindergarten settings and most teachers are quite knowledgeable about the wealth of excellent literature available. These are the primary reasons teachers often find story dramatization the easiest place to begin. Not only are the characters and plot ready-made, but most children's stories cover themes pertinent to early childhood learning and are integrated regularly into preschool–kindergarten curricula. Drama can clarify these themes for young children as they "step into the action," providing opportunities to deepen their level of thinking.

Story Drama Methodology

The story dramas that follow are listed under three categories of story drama methodology: storytime drama, linear story drama, and extended story drama. Yet even within these specific approaches, there is a range of dramatic activity, flexibility, and levels of involvement, as described in the previous chapter.

STORYTIME DRAMA

In this approach, drama is integrated into the actual storytime. The aim of all three sessions reported under this category is to enhance story comprehension and pique interest, in addition to other class-specific objectives. It is possible to vary each drama session to emphasize other objectives.

If a teacher is interested in emphasizing a particular aspect of the story, it is quite simple to stop in the middle of reading (before or after will do as well) and ask children to imagine that they are a character in the story. This technique also provides a secure outline for a teacher new

40

to drama, with the safety of the story circle for the children to come back to. It usually works best to have all children play the same character, or character type, simultaneously.

Though the drama sessions reported in this chapter cover most scenes of the story, it is not necessary to dramatize a story in its entirety. Drama can be used in short sessions to highlight one scene of a story or to explore one specific character. A five- to fifteen-minute drama treatment of one aspect of the story is an excellent way for teachers to begin integrating drama into language arts and storytime activities.

LINEAR STORY DRAMA

We are using the term *linear story dramatization* to describe process-oriented drama that follows the story sequentially. Linear should not be taken as a hard and fast rule, as the drama must have flexibility to extend beyond the boundaries of the story when children's curiosity and interest demand. You may even choose to go backward or forward in time. It is also important to note that, though the drama may follow the sequence of the story, children are not acting it out as a play.

The linear story drama sessions that follow are broken down into scenes, or steps, of the story that are explored individually. For example, in *Caps for Sale* children might spend a good amount of time setting up a village and exploring roles and jobs for the villagers that will try on the capseller's caps. They also might improvise monkey movement and behavior. Neither of these is actually part of the story, but they provide an opportunity for the children to explore the characters and events more fully.

EXTENDED STORY DRAMA

A further, more ambitious strategy is using drama to extend a story over three or more sessions. By integrating storytelling with a range of dramatic possibilities, a book such as *The Mud Pony, Where The Wild Things Are*, or *The Giant Jam Sandwich* can turn into a week-long project, enlivening and incorporating other curriculum units as well as parts of the daily routine. Snack becomes Max's supper; baking the bread for the jam sandwich becomes a lesson not only in breadmaking, but also in counting, measuring, and timing as well as nutrition. Furthermore, Max's journey prepares the way for a discussion about dreams and nightmares (see Chapter 6).

Though the extended story dramatizations in this chapter appear planned, much of the work evolved from the responses and expressed interests of the children.

READING THE STORY BEFORE OR AFTER DRAMA

Most of the story dramas in this chapter were presented to children before they actually knew the story. Though there are some situations in which you may want to read a story first. (For example, a story that involves disturbing elements should be told in its entirety to settle any uncertainy in the child's mind about a happy resolution.) There are benefits to dramatizing a story at least once *before* it is read out loud:

- Dramatizing before reading the story allows the teacher to reduce the events and characters for clarity. Once children have explored the major concepts through drama, they will be more receptive to following the ins and outs of the plot when the book is read in its entirety. This time, however, their listening skills, comprehension, and recall will be much sharper.
- Dramatizing before reading piques children's interest in printed materials. Once they have lived firsthand through Brave Irene's adventures in the snowstorm or expressed Max's feelings on returning home, children want to see the pictures and read (or be read to) about that same experience.
- By dramatizing the story before it is read, children's imaginations are not limited by the pictures and specifics of the book. For example, when asked to imagine what a "Wild Thing" might look like before seeing Maurice Sendak's vivid depiction, children as young as three have given such creative answers as "bubble fur," "one large eye spinning on top of its head," and "a curly nose." Later, children enjoy comparing their dramatized version of the story with the illustrated book. Don't hesitate to change the gender of the protagonist. Stories with dynamic plots suited for drama tend to have male protagonists; it may be helpful to counterpoint this early stereotyping.

Story Drama Reports

Following are seven reports of actual story drama sessions and extended story drama work. These examples come from preschool and kindergarten classrooms. There are also five abbreviated story dramas that leave room for teachers to flex their creative muscles and develop material of their own. Notice how each story drama:

- provides a clear introduction and closing
- is a series of short scenes or segments

- engages all the children in role simultaneously
- varies the level of involvement and type of dramatic activity
- limits turn taking and observation of others' work.

Story dramas that work particularly well with early threes (and some older twos) are marked with a [3]. Additionally, all of the drama work in Chapter Eight is well suited for early threes. Please remember that children as old as six also enjoy this simpler drama work.

In spite of the detail and some teacher narrative, these dramatizations should not be considered scripts. Each report is followed by a list of choices other teachers have made when using drama to explore the same story. If you are interested in using this material in your own classroom, it is our hope is that you will feel free to make whatever adaptations you deem necessary.[1]

STORYTIME DRAMA SESSIONS

In the following sessions, drama is integrated into reading the story out loud. The first story, *So Much,* is quite simple, created for a small group of three-year-old children. The second and third stories are treated more fully, drama accentuating each main event. Many of the individual activities within these storytime dramas also work well alone to underscore a particular point in the story.

So Much [3]
From the book by Trish Cooke, illustrated by Helen Oxenbury

This story works best with a small group of three- and early four-year-old children. It is a melodic tale of mother and baby home alone until all the relatives come by to visit, one by one, for a surprise party for daddy. They all give the baby so much love.

Before Reading the Story The teacher gives each child a doll or stuffed animal to be their baby. She lets the children take care of their baby for a bit, then asks them what they think babies like to do. Using the dolls, they pantomime some of their ideas (clapping, crying, and singing).

Stopping for Drama As each relative arrives in the story, the teacher stops to add dramatic action, starting with Auntie Bibba. The children become Auntie Bibba, hugging and squeezing their baby so much, and playing "clap-clap" for a short while. This is repeated for Uncle Didi, kissing the baby and playing "flip-flap," Nannie and Gran-Gran making him feel so cozy, and so on. After acting out the second character in the story, the children begin to initiate the acting out on their own. Throughout most of the action, the children remain seated in a circle.

Closing As the story ends, children put their babies to bed. Then the teacher becomes the mother and the children become all her babies, going to bed. She rubs their backs and tells them how they are loved by their mommies, daddies, grannies, gramps, uncles, aunts, and cousins, and teacher . . . so much!

Other Teachers Made These Choices

- Brought in various baby props for the children to touch, smell, and listen to, such as lullabies, rattle sounds, baby powder, soft "blankies," and cuddly toys.
- Read the story to five or six children at a time, allowing one to hold the baby and the others to become the characters, each with a special hat.

STELLALUNA [3]
From the story by Janell Cannon

This is a story about separations and reunions as well as similarities and differences.

Materials Surgical gloves and soft feathers.

Before the Story After sharing pictures of bats and reviewing the previous days' bat discussion, the teacher gives each child two surgical gloves, telling them they're going to use them to make bats. (The gloves suggest the texture and elastic quality of a bat's wing.) Before putting them on, she has the class flap their "bat wings" in unison, using a high-pitched whistle for the bat call. After this, she and her aide help the children put the gloves on. They choose between joining hands to make one bat puppet or keeping hands separate as two bat puppets. She demonstrates both, then gives them time to create their own "flying bats."

Stopping for Drama After Stellaluna and her mother are separated, the teacher stops reading and asks the children to mime this action with their bat puppets. Most verbalize the separation with cries like "Mama, help me, I'm falling," whereas some prefer nonverbal "bat squeaks." The action ends with the teacher showing the picture of Stellaluna hanging upside down alone, the "bats" copying her pose.

- The story continues, with Stellaluna falling into the birds' nest, then being taken in and fed with baby bird food. The teacher stops to let her brood of "bats" (portrayed by the children this time) open their mouths, close their eyes, and try some "grasshoppers" (chunks of celery) and "worms" (spaghetti).

- The teacher pauses again for puppet play after reading about Stellaluna hanging "upside down"(right way up for a bird and a person) and meeting a bat hanging "the right way up" (upside down for a bird and a person). Some children have difficulty conceptualizing this, so they act it out with their own bodies first.
- Finally, they stop to act out the emotional reunion of Stellaluna and her mother. The teacher asks how the bats felt. "Better" one child says; "And the Mommy too," another chimes in. The teacher completes the story, offering each "bat" a "baby bird friend" (feathers in a wicker nest) to hug.

Closing Bird nests are collected and children take off their "bat skins," rubbing their skin until it feels soft and human, not stretchy and batlike.

Follow-up The teacher reads Janell Cannon's follow-up information about fruit bats.

Other Teachers Made These Choices

- Only stopped in two places, letting children make hand/sign puppets to create dialogue between the bat and bird, then later between Stellaluna and her mother.
- Sliced up a ripe mango and gave every child-bat a taste.
- Made a cave out of cloth and hung the surgical gloves inside, taking dictation as the children took turns exploring the cave.

BRAVE IRENE
From the story by William Steig

This is a story about a girl who braves the cold and dark to deliver a party dress made by her mother.

Materials Ice, flashlight, swatches of different colored and textured cloth.

Before the Story The teacher asks children what the word *brave* means. Several make "tough" faces and flex their muscles. "That's brave on the outside," the teacher says, and continues, "To be truly brave you have to be brave on the inside as well. Let's all find our brave hearts." Everyone beats their chest. "Let's close our eyes and find a brave place in our imaginations." After they've had time to concentrate, the teacher tells them that today's story is about a girl who is both brave on the outside and on the inside.

Stopping for Drama

- As Irene prepares to leave her mother's house, children mime putting on winter clothes for the journey. The teacher elicits

- -

suggestions from them as to what kind of clothes they'll need for wintry weather. She passes ice around the circle so everyone can feel the cold outside. They then either pick up or mime picking up the precious box.

■ As she reads, the teacher dramatizes the wind's voice. After each page of the trip, they mime Irene's battles with the wind and weather.

■ When the dress blows away, the teacher asks a child to "spot" it in the classroom. All point, pretending to see it. They "watch" the dress flying back and forth until it disappears into the distance.

The teacher asks how Irene is feeling. "Bad," some say. "Worried that her mother will be angry," another says. The teacher stresses Irene remembering her mother's loving face and how much she loves Irene—it's love, not fear, that motivates her.

■ When Irene becomes lost, the teacher darkens the room, using a flashlight to make the moon. Then, dancing flashlights are used to make the palace lights. The children beat their hearts to create Irene's brave heart, and close their eyes to see what "answer" they can come up with themselves, before the box-sled solution is revealed in the book.

■ When Irene recovers the dress, the teacher brings out her box of fabrics and lets each child pick their own swatch to make a party dress for the Duchess. She then asks each child what makes their dress special. "Mine's a happy dress because it's got polka dots," says one. "Mine's red and warm, like a fire fighter's coat," says another. "Mine's shiny and good for dancing in," says a third. (This is one way of giving children an opportunity to make an individual contribution to the drama.)

■ Inside the palace, the teacher puts on a glittering tiara and becomes the Duchess distributing cookies. After the party scene, each child stands and mimes dancing, holding their party dress in front of them and moving to dance music.

Closing At the end of the story, the teacher becomes Irene's mother and tucks each "Irene" into bed, telling her what a brave and loving child she's been, how proud she is to be her mother.

Follow-up Each child makes their own dress by gluing pieces of material onto an outline of a dress on a piece of construction paper. Decorations, such as glitter and sequins, are added to make it a special party dress.

Other Teachers Made These Choices

- Made the textured dresses first to get a sense of the care the mother took in making the Duchess dress.
- Paired children up as Irene and her mother. The "Irenes" told the "mothers" all about their adventure. "Mothers" expressed what they were feeling and doing at home while Irene was battling the elements. This sparked a discussion about what to do if you're lost.
- Used a hand-held fan to blow "wind" on each child's face (and another time used crepe streamers).

LINEAR STORY DRAMA SESSIONS

Though these reported drama sessions follow the story somewhat sequentially, there were diversions along the way to accommodate children's needs and responses.

LANCE THE GIRAFFE [3]
By Victoria Brown

This is a story about a giraffe who desperately wants to be different until he discovers his own special self.

Introduction The aim of this session was to foster language use and self esteem and to encourage problem solving. This drama also highlights the use of integrating sign language (see Chapter 4). Signs are used to create characters and setting, keeping the children involved, with very little movement outside the circle.

The teacher tells the children that they will use drama to tell a story about a giraffe named Lance. Using giraffe pictures, she points out specific features: "Lance looked just like all the other giraffes. He had big eyes, little ears, a little tail, long legs, a long neck, spots all over his body, and a long tongue he used to pull the leaves off of trees."

Children create a giraffe, using their arm as the neck, and their hand as the puppet head. Their giraffe hand-puppets eat leaves from a tree they create with their opposite arm and hand.

Children then become giraffes, using hand shapes to create features of the giraffe on their own bodies, including Lance's long tongue to reach leaves from trees. One child looks around at the imaginary spots and remarks, "Hey, we look like Dalmatians!" They stretch their necks up high, pretending to eat leaves from imaginary trees.

Part One Back in the circle, the teacher narrates the beginning of the story, with the children following along using signs. "Lance was tired of just being an ordinary giraffe. He wanted to be different. He wanted to be special. You know what Lance wanted to do? He wanted to climb a tree like a squirrel." A picture of a squirrel is shown. Children shape one hand like a squirrel and the other like a tree, moving the hand-squirrel up the hand-tree.

"Lance wanted to fly like a bird and swim like a fish." Again, pictures of a bird and fish are shown, with children creating flying birds and swimming fish with their hands.

"When Lance told the other giraffes about his dreams, they laughed." Creating two hand-giraffes, children act out the scenario, adding laughter and dialogue between the two characters.

"One day, when all the other giraffes went off to eat leaves from trees, Lance decided he would try to climb a tree like a squirrel." Children use one hand to create a tree and the other as Lance climbing a bit until he falls. "Owwwwwwww!," the teacher calls out, holding her toe, "Lance hurt his toe! How could a giraffe walk with a sore toe. Show me." Standing, they all become Lance, trying out different ways of limping, hopping, and moaning. At first they all imitate one very demonstrative child, but the teacher encourages creativity by side coaching, "I notice a different way of moving . . . ." This motivates many to try something new.

"Here come those other giraffes," the teacher calls, as a means of gathering children into the circle. "What do you think the giraffes will say when they see Lance?" Children, with arms and hands as giraffe puppets, create the dialogue. Many of the Lance hand puppets cry.

Part Two Lance's endeavor to be different continues. This time he tries flying. Children bring knees up to form a hill and, using their hand as the giraffe, climb the hill. As they count to three, Lance jumps off flapping his legs, but falls to the ground, hurting his neck. Soon they are up, limping around the circle with a sore toe *and* a sore neck—moaning mixed with giggles. Back to the circle again, hand-giraffes carry out another dialogue. Again, Lance cries. (The repetition of the scenario helps the children feel confident with the drama. They become more verbal and quite involved by the third time around, when they are asked to problem solve.)

Part Three Children form a circle with their legs, making a lake. Hand-fish swim around. On the count of three, Lance (hand puppet), hoping to swim, jumps into the water and becomes stuck in the mud. Children are now encouraged to come up with a solution for getting Lance out of the water. Ideas include the fish pushing him out and an elephant pulling him out with its trunk. The teacher has the children act out as many of their ideas as possible. Finally, they rescue Lance.

"Ahhh, Ahhh, Choooooo! Uh oh, Lance caught a cold from that cold water." Standing, they become Lance again, moving about with sore toe, sore neck, and lots of sneezing. After a few minutes, they return to the circle, creating the hand-puppet dialogue with the other giraffes.

Part Four "The next day, when all the other giraffes were gone, Lance stayed home, feeling sad. Then, suddenly he heard music. (Any music that is good for dancing will do here.) Lance looked all around, but he couldn't see anything. Then he looked down to see that his foot was tapping, then another foot, and soon all four feet were tapping. Lance was dancing! He *was* special—the only dancing giraffe!"

Children make their giraffe hand puppets dance, then spontaneously offer dialogue from the other giraffes, who are impressed with Lance's new found talent. Finally, they are up creating their own giraffe dance as they celebrate Lance's discovery.

Closing All pretend to scrub off their spots and other giraffe features, becoming children again. They share ways in which they are special, such as tying shoes all by themselves, blowing a bubble, or whistling.

Other Teachers Made These Choices

- Gave one child in a mainstreamed classroom the special role of becoming Lance's friend (a wise monkey), who clapped two blocks together to warn Lance that the other giraffes were returning. Physically disabled children participated throughout by using their hand-puppet characters.
- Brought in small branches with fresh leaves for the children to smell—then held the branches above the children's heads as they stretched to be as tall as a giraffe.
- Let children add colored giraffe spots to their faces with washable face paint (part of the celebration "giraffe dance").

BREAD AND HONEY
From the book by Frank Asch

In this story, Ben makes a picture of his mother at school but changes it to satisfy the six animals he meets on his way home. The aim of the drama is to foster language use, social skills, and group cooperation.

Materials Paper plates, construction paper, and so on, for mask making, a simple hand-drawn picture of a woman's face (Ben's mother), and bread and honey for a closing snack.

Preparation The day before the dramatization, children make simple paper plate masks to use for the story drama. There are six animals in this story: an owl with big eyes, an alligator with a large mouth, a rabbit with long ears, an elephant with long trunk, a lion with long mane, and a giraffe with a long neck. Identifying features are cut from construction paper (a paper towel tube for the elephant's trunk) and stapled onto the paper plate. Other features are added with markers and paper scraps.

Introduction Children look at pictures and explore each animal's features, sounds, and movement. (This could be done the day before the drama.) They are told that they will be acting out a story about a child named Ben who meets lots of different animals.

Part One Children are divided into pairs. One in each pair is the little boy (or girl) and one is the mother (or father). Each pair improvises a short scene of a parent waking up a child in the morning. "Who wakes you up in the morning? Show me how." They awaken, washing faces, dressing, eating breakfast, brushing teeth, and so forth.

The teacher narrates: "In this story there is a little boy named Ben. When Ben wakes up in the morning and gets ready for school, he smells the bread his mother is baking in the oven. "Mothers (or fathers), can you pretend you are baking bread?" The teacher encourages them to ask for some bread. "Ben's mother says 'The bread is too hot now. But you can have some when you come home from school.' And Ben asks, 'With honey on top?' and his mother answers, 'Yes, with lots of honey on top.'" Children repeat this dialogue and then say goodbye to their parents, as they pretend to leave for school.

Note: If this dramatization is done in two days, take time to repeat part one with the children in reverse roles. Tell them they will finish the story next time, becoming all of the different animals that Ben meets on his way home from school. When you begin the drama the second day, review the movement and major features of the animals as an introduction.

Part Two Gathering into a circle, the teacher explains that when Ben went to school that day, he painted a picture of his mother. She shows them the picture of Ben's mother (predrawn), then selects a volunteer to play the role of Ben. The others are divided into the six animal groups, with three or four children acting out the same animal. (They wear the masks around their necks, to help everyone identify the animals).[2]

Ben is led down the road back home from school. As he walks by each group of animals, he asks, "Do you like this picture of my mother I made in school today?" The owl likes the picture but complains that the eyes are too small. Ben (or one of the owls) changes the drawing, adding big owl eyes. The alligator thinks the mouth is too small, and so on. (Some children need prompting when responding to Ben.) Each time Ben talks to a different group of animals, they change the picture accordingly.

Part Three By the time Ben arrives home, the mother's picture has big eyes, mouth, nose, and ears, and long hair and neck. The teacher puts on an apron, becoming Ben's mother. She tells Ben that she loves the picture just the way it is and hangs it on the refrigerator. Ben is told he can invite all his animal friends home for some bread with lots of honey on top.

Closing All gather around the tables for bread and honey. After cleaning up, they go back into the parent–child pairs and have the child portraying Ben recall his meeting with the animals. After a few minutes they switch roles, giving each child an opportunity for recall.

Follow-up Many children from this group want to draw their own funny pictures with animal features. Some draw pictures of their mother or caretaker to take home.

Other Teachers Made These Choices

- Simplified this story by reducing the number of animals that Ben visits and by keeping the characters within the circle. A clear separation of each animal category was made, using masking tape to mark the animals' habitats.
- Allowed two children to portray Ben and his sister.
- Simplified mask making by letting three-year-old children select and glue on precut features of the animals.
- Instead of pairing up the children at the end, one teacher stayed in the mother role, letting children recall the journey to her.
- Made bread with the children as a follow-up.

WHERE THE WILD THINGS ARE
From the book by Maurice Sendak

A children's classic about a young boy named Max who journeys far from home to discover he is truly loved, wildness and all. The drama work can be adapted to facilitate a wide range of learning objectives. In this particular session, the teacher wanted to enhance the children's use of descriptive language.

Material Strips of furry material for wolf tails, jungle pictures, dolls.

Introduction Gathered into a circle, children are told they will be dramatizing a story about wild things (some have seen the book, but not all). The teacher asks what they think wild things could be, what they might look like and what they might do. Some mention tigers, lions, and wolves as wild things.

Standing, they become imaginary Wild Things, adding on exaggerated features with hand shapes as if they were putting on costume pieces: ears, nose, eyes, teeth, horns, fur, claws, and so on. Creativity is encouraged, and anything goes. (One child creates "bubblegum fur," another has "one big eye on top of his head that spins around.") Then they move like Wild Things, jumping, swinging from trees, marching, and dancing—all within the circle.

Note: This part of the drama can continue for a good long while and serve as the first day of a three-day plan, perhaps letting the children paint pictures of their Wild Thing creations as a closing for the first session.

Part One: *Making Mischief* Teacher narration: "There is a boy in this story who sometimes acts very wild. His name is Max. Max sometimes gets into trouble with his mother when he is acting wild and making mischief. Have you ever gotten in trouble for doing something wild in your home?" They talk about what this means. The children are initially shy, so the teacher gives examples of wild things she used to do that caused her mother to get very angry. Finally, they take turns talking about their own mischievous deeds. One child has recently thrown her sister's shoe in the toilet. This gets such a big response, they act it out, pretending to flush a shoe down a toilet, with wonderful sound effects.

The teacher continues: "One night, Max was really mischievous and put on a wolf costume and made some terrible mischief." She hands them each a "wolf tail" (strips of furry material). They mime putting on the rest of the costume using hand shapes to define such wolf features as long snout, sharp teeth, and ears. "In the book, Max is a boy, but in your imaginations Max can be a girl or a boy," the teacher tells them. Then all mime "making mischief," including ideas from their earlier discussion, such as jumping on the bed and throwing shoes. This is all done within the confines of the circle.

Part Two: *Max's Mother* The teacher explains to them what will happen next: "When Max's mother saw what Max was doing, she got very angry! Now I'm going to be Max's mother and get angry at you. When I put this scarf around my head, I will be Max's mother. You will all be Max jumping on the bed and making lots of noise." She pretends to walk down the stairs and turns her back to them. After a short period of their jumping and shouting, she turns back around, "Max certainly is making a lot of noise upstairs. I better go up there and see what he's doing! Max! What are you doing? You Wild Thing!" Then (speaking as the teacher again), "But Max didn't listen. He told his mom he was going to eat her up." They repeat this part of the story a few times, yelling, "I'll eat you up," then the teacher returns to the mother role, responding with, "You go to your room without your supper!"

With the teacher's guidance, the children sit in a circle, pretending that they are in their bedroom sitting on their bed.

Part Three: *Room Transformation* With the teacher leading, children use gestures to depict the transformation of the room, adding grass, trees, vines, and an ocean surrounding them. They use their hands to create a boat that sails "through night and day and almost over a year to where the Wild Things are." They are asked what they think Max might have seen while crossing the ocean, and they make that animal or object with one hand, interacting with the other "hand-boat." One child makes an octopus, another a shark floating under the boat, another a sea gull flying over the boat, and so on. One child spots an elephant and the teacher supports this by saying, "What a great imagination Max has!"

After a bit of calm sailing, the hand-boat bumps into an island (children use knees to make a hill for this place). "Walking fingers" represent Max climbing out of the boat and onto the land.

Note: If extending this drama for three days, stop here to complete the second day. Follow up with water play or finger painting. One class used a garden hose to create a lake in the sand box, with an island in the middle.

Part Four: *Max's Arrival* Because the location of the story has changed, the teacher spends a few minutes describing the setting by showing some jungle pictures and having the children use gestures to create the trees and vines. At this point in the drama, children also change roles. They transform into Wild Things by using hand shapes once again to add on the features, as in the introduction, including types of fur, scales, feathers, and so on.

The teacher uses a stuffed doll to represent the character of Max. This creates a feeling for the "Wild Things" of being very large, looking down at Max as the teacher mimes him climbing out of his boat and looking up at the Wild Things. Other possibilities include having the teacher take on the role of Max or using an assistant or puppet to portray this role.

With prompting, the Wild Things roar wildly, gnash their teeth, roll their eyes, and show their long claws. The teacher responds, "You know what Max did? He said 'Be still!' and tamed them by staring into their eyes without blinking. Let's try that. When Max looks at you, you must freeze!" The Max doll "tames" them, and when all are "frozen" in place, the teacher has them sit quietly. Max is crowned king of all Wild Things.

Part Five: *Rumpus Making* Now, Max the king, leads children into some rumpus making—jumping, swinging from imaginary trees, marching, and dancing. The entire room is used for this (could parade down the hall, or outside, if possible). They are then sent to bed without their supper, lying down and pretending to sleep.

As the children pretend to sleep, the next part of the story is narrated very softly, describing Max's loneliness: "Max started to leave, but the Wild Things cried, 'Oh please don't go—we'll eat you up—we love you so!'" The Wild Things are asked to sit up and repeat the response to

Max. They also repeat roaring, gnashing, eye rolling, and claw showing, *seated,* as Max waves good-bye and sails away.

Part Six: *Back Home* Children change roles back to Max by rubbing off their Wild Thing features. They make a boat again with their hands and sail back home as the teacher narrates Max back to his own room.

Closing Children are now seated in the circle. "Do you know what Max found in his very own room? His supper, and it was still warm." They mime taking off their wolf costume (while still seated) and discuss what Max's mother might have brought for dinner. Then, pretending to eat, they talk about their own favorite foods, making the transition back to the classroom.

Discussion These are some of the questions that were asked: What part of the drama did you like best? Was it more fun being Max or a Wild Thing? Why do you think Max's mother brought him his dinner? Do you think Max will ever visit the Wild Things again? This is also an opportunity to validate students' emotional responses to discipline without undermining a parent or teacher's right to enforce limits: Was being sent to bed a fair punishment, and if not, what else might have been effective? This enables them, in an objective way, to understand the value and logic of discipline beyond its merely subjective affect.

Follow-up The story is read and children make comparisons between their imagined Wild Things and the author's illustrations, and then discuss other ways the book and dramatized story differed.

Other Teachers Made These Choices

- Created another Max adventure, asking children to imagine what other wonderful places Max could travel to in his boat, then dramatized some of these journeys.
- When children became overstimulated by parts of this drama, "rumpus making" was simplified by keeping children within the circle and establishing a clear control for the action. The Wild Things were allowed to "act wild" until Max blinked the lights off and on, at which point they had to freeze in place.
- Controlled "rumpus making" by creating and leading a follow-the-leader Rumpus Parade.
- One class of children with special needs had difficulty imagining the events in the drama. The book was read first, showing Sendak's pictures, then read again, stopping to act out some key events.
- Extended the drama over three sessions, focusing on the emotional and psychological aspects of this story (see Chapter 6).

EXTENDED STORY DRAMA

The following extended dramatization uses drama to explore a story over several sessions. The story is told first, then retold at the beginning of each new session.

THE MUD PONY
From the book by Caron Lee Cohen

This is a story about a poor boy who finds solace by making a pony out of mud. When the boy is left behind by his tribe, the mud pony returns as a dream pony and finally as a real one to bring the boy back home. This extended drama is divided into five sessions covering five separate days.

DAY ONE

Objective To introduce the children to Native American cultures, specifically the Pawnee of the American Plains.

Materials Pictures of Pawnee natives, teepees, and buffalo; musk powder or perfume; blankets.

Introduction Children prepare for the drama work with an introduction to the Pawnee tribe. This first session focuses on becoming a tribe. The teacher begins, "We are going to tell a story that was told by the first people who walked this American soil, the Pawnee people. Clap out the syllables Paw-nee with me. The Pawnee people were buffalo hunters." The teacher shows them pictures of buffalo. There is some brief discussion about buffalo hunting, which leads into the storytelling.

Storytelling The teacher narrates the story of a boy who was hungry and longed for a pony of his own like the other boys. Instead of reading from the book (which was done later), she tells it more simply in her own words. (Either way, it may be preferable to tell the story only as far as the boy's return to the tribe, omitting the battle, as it reinforces negative stereotypes about warlike "Indians.")

She describes the pony (mud, dream, and real) as having a "long flowing mane, long, straight legs, and a tail that moved from side to side." She repeats this each time, with simple gestures.

Drama Using desks, tables, sheets, and blankets, the children create teepees in different parts of the classroom. Some work together in pairs or groups of threes, and others create their own private tents. Then all come together to prepare for a buffalo hunt (or, if time has run out, a meal).

- Each child listens, ear to the ground, for the buffalo sound or vibration. The teacher becomes the chief, directing the hunt, while taking suggestions from the children. This keeps the class together as a group. She maintains a sense of ritual by having them periodically listen to the earth to locate the buffalo, reminding them of the importance of silence during a hunt. Occasionally, children smell "buffalo scent" (musk-scented perfume), letting them know they are on course.

■ They mime shooting the buffalo, bringing it home, and cooking the meat over a fire. Before the meal, they perform the ritual of thanking the buffalo for feeding the people. The teacher uses a large wool blanket to represent the buffalo.

Closing The teacher gathers the tribe around the embers of the campfire, wrapping each of the "Pawnees" in a blanket to sleep. As the children "sleep," they rub off their Pawnee selves and return to being children in the classroom. These blankets will be used for the rest of the dramatizations.

DAY TWO

Materials Lemon, popcorn, butcher paper, washtub of water, and chocolate pudding.

Objective To introduce the concept of hunger and how it can be satisfied through creative and imaginative experiences as well as by literal food.

Introduction Gathered in a circle, the drama begins with a discussion of "hunger." The teacher asks the children what hunger feels like, and which parts of the body feel it the most. Each child receives a squeeze of lemon juice, to stimulate the taste of hunger. They discuss and describe this sensation. The teacher suggests that there are things other than food that excite this feeling. She asks the children what other things they want so badly they feel hungry just thinking about them—possibly possessions owned by other children that they don't have themselves. Many talk about specific toys. One child mentions friends and another, parents (no wrong or right answers here).

Storytelling The story is retold, focusing on the boy's hunger as it applies both to food and to his friends' possessions, especially their ponies. The teacher illustrates the family's poverty by giving them popcorn as the only available food. They discuss the dry, empty sensation it creates—a food that can't satisfy.

Drama The boy's trip to the stream is acted out with every child playing the boy. They follow the sound of the stream (could be a water tape or a trail of popcorn to follow). The teacher has set out plastic tubs of water (on sheets of newspaper) for a tactile representation of the stream, and the children squat around them and move their hands through the water. In this way, they experience "the stream" *and* wash up, ready to work with food.

- In another area of the room, sheets of butcher paper have been laid out, with pony outlines predrawn, one for each child. The teacher calls them to the tables, and they fill in the outlines with chocolate-pudding "mud." A few minutes into the exercise, most of the children have wised up to the fact that "the mud" is edible, but the teacher urges them to keep drawing until they've finished making their ponies. Now they can taste the satisfaction of creating a pony from their imagination, picking up the notion—if only on a subliminal level—that creativity can satisfy that inner hunger, "that sour taste." When they're done, she spoons the left over pudding into cups and lets everyone enjoy it.
- They return to the "stream" again and wash off the pudding before gathering again at the campfire.

Closing Children are wrapped in their warm blankets. The teacher shines the moon (flashlight) on each child, then "sparkles" the light with a prism crystal held over the beam. As the starlight sparkles, she narrates the promise that the boy *will* find his family once again, just as the class *will* return to their classroom, their teachers, and the rest of their day.

DAY THREE

Objective To develop the vocabulary for dreams, differentiate dreams from reality, and appreciate their power.

Materials Yarn, mud in a double zip-lock bag, popcorn, cotton balls, bells, bubbles, blankets, an overhead projector, and an overhead acetate of a pony.

Introduction Children are gathered into a circle to create a yarn dream catcher (see *The Very Busy Spider* [Chapter 7] for directions). As they are weaving, children talk about what dreams are and describe their own. The teacher blows bubbles over the dream catcher to demonstrate how it lets the good ones through and keeps the bad out: "But in the end, dreams all pop, because dreams are different from the real world, just as many stories are."

Storytelling As the teacher retells the story, she integrates some of yesterday's props, such as the popcorn and the bells. Instead of chocolate pudding, she uses real mud (in a double zip-lock bag) for the children to feel. In this telling, the emphasis is on the feelings of loneliness and sadness the boy experienced as he went to sleep, and how they were transformed by the visit from the dream pony.

Drama Each child is given their blanket. As a group, they use the blankets to create their dream or sleeping space in the room. The lights are shut off, and the teacher plays "dream" music, giving each child dream eyes (a piece of red or blue acetate to look through). She blows bubbles over the children to create the illusion of dream ponies.

Closing For closure, the teacher projects the image of a pony onto the ceiling through an overhead projector, using a red acetate cutout. They use cotton balls as pillows, and then use them to rub the dreams away.

DAY FOUR

Objective To move beyond the imaginative and visionary aspects of the story into the literal experience of the hero journey.

Materials Hair dryer, sage or an earthy incense, backpacks, blue cloth, granola, hand-drawn map, rocks or small blocks for horses' hooves, face paint, and mask of "the spirit of Mother Earth."

Introduction The teacher warms up each child by having them feel the pony's breath on their faces and cheeks (hair dryer). Each child privately names their individual pony friend. She lights stems of dried sage to let each child smell the smoke from the tribe's distant campfire, saying, "The wind has blown this toward you to guide you on your journey."

They gather around a map of the route from the old campfire to the new one. This includes the mountains and rivers they will have to cross to reach their final destination.

Storytelling This time, as the teacher retells the story, every child holds a rock in each hand to make "hoof sounds." They beat out the various stages of their journey: trotting, cantering, galloping, climbing and descending, then finally slowing down.

Drama In this session, children become the ponies. The teacher streaks their noses with black or brown face paint. A wet pony nose is made with a dab of lip gloss. Each child wears a backpack (packed with books, etc.) to feel the weight of the boy on their backs. They are led on a journey up mountains and along precipices (taped lines), across rivers (blue cloth) and galloping over plains. The classroom journey imitates the journey on the map.

The ponies stop to eat and drink from streams (cups of fresh water and a handful of pony food—granola). Returning to the circle, they imagine the remainder of the trip back to the tribe and the boy's joyous reunion with the tribe. Children take off the back packs and hand the "boys" over to the "parents." The teacher announces, "The ponies are very tired and need to rest so they can complete the journey home tomorrow."

Closing The teacher gives each child a cotton ball soaked in a little water and guides them as they rub off their pony noses and pony selves and return to being children.

Follow-up Children create their own maps of the journey they've just taken in the drama.

DAY FIVE

Objective To review the story and reach closure.

Material Parachute and art materials.

Storytelling Gathered in a circle, children are encouraged to tell as much of the story as they can, putting it in their own words. The teacher takes dictation. (Later, she writes up their version for them to illustrate and keep.) She reminds the children that the pony stayed with the boy in his heart and that the boy grew to be like the pony, with "long flowing hair, long, straight legs and eyes that swished from side to side, and he grew strong, brave and wise but always with a gentle, loving heart."

Drama This session focuses on the end of the journey and the homecoming. The children all portray the boy, getting closer and closer to home. With adult help, they create a huge tent, using a billowed parachute. Each time the parachute billows, the teacher asks, "Can you see the tent yet?" Finally, when the parachute has sufficient volume, the teacher and "boys" sit underneath it. Outside "the tent" the aide quickly wraps herself in a blanket to assume the role of the boy's parent. She slips under the tent and greets her "sons" bidding each "to lie down and rest now after your long journey."

As "the tent" is lifted off, the teacher encourages them to embrace their "dream ponies." They feel for their own heartbeats, and she tells them that the ponies' hooves are still beating in their hearts.

Closing Once again, the teacher wraps them back in their blankets and this time sends them to "sleep" by rubbing their backs, singing, "I am the spirit of Mother Earth. I will never leave you." She tells them it is now time to let go of the old story and return to the classroom.

Follow-up Choosing colors, paints, or clay, children illustrate their own version of the story. The teacher reads the children's versions out loud during storytime.

Other Teachers Made These Choices:

- In a mainstreamed classroom, a miniature puppet show, using toys and simple props, was used to clarify the plot. Much of the activity was done seated, using plastic Easter egg halves to make the horse's hooves sound, instead of having the children gallop around the room. Pictures from the book were shown throughout the drama to help children follow the story.

- For the dream sequence, half of the children became dream ponies and wove in among the sleepers; then they switched roles.

Suggestions for More Story Dramatization

The following story dramas summarize and combine choices different teachers made when working with the stories. They are presented in abbreviated form as a starting point for teachers to begin creating their own plans for drama. We recommend that you adhere to the structure of introduction, dramatization of the steps of the story, and closure.

STORYTIME DRAMA

MIRANDY AND BROTHER WIND
From the book by Patricia C. McKissack, illustrated by Jerry Pinkney

Mirandy wants Brother Wind to be her dance partner at the cakewalk. She follows several neighbors' suggestions for capturing the wind, while her friend Ezel laughs at each blunder. In the end, she surprises everyone.

Materials A fan, various materials to "float in the wind," and streamers.

Before Reading the Story You might explore the wind outdoors on a windy day, or create your own wind in the classroom with fans. Let different types of material float in the wind. Children can also create wind with their bodies: soft, strong, and spinning wind.

Stopping for Drama After Mirandy has tried one or two of her neighbors' suggestions for capturing the wind, stop the story and ask the children for their suggestions—how might *they* capture the wind? If there is time, dramatize one or more of their ideas, using real or imaginary props.

Once Mirandy has captured the wind, stop before the book reveals her plan. Give children scarves, streamers, or strips of thin material and let them create a wind dance.

Closing Divide the children into pairs—Mirandy recalling her journey of capturing the wind to her friend, Ezel.

Other Choices

- Use a hand-held fan to blow on each child, initiating their dance.
- Select music to represent the wind and guide their wind dance, fading it out as the wind dies down.

- Create a cakewalk dance, perhaps inviting parents to join.
- Let the children create their own dramas: how to capture a rainbow, the sun, the moon, and clouds.

Tops and Bottoms [3]
From the book adapted and illustrated by Janet Stevens

In this beautifully illustrated trickster tale, a lazy bear with lots of land is fooled by a hungry hare with a large family and a clever plan.

Before the Story Consider various ways for the children to compare and explore the vegetables represented in the story.

Stopping for Drama Perhaps a stuffed bear could be used to represent Mr. Bear, and the children could become Mr. Hare's children.
Each time the garden is planted, stop and let the hares act out digging weeds, planting, and watering.

Closing Perhaps the hares could teach the Bear-puppet how to plant. He could give each child a bear hug as thanks.

Other Choices

- Make a salad out of "tops" and a salad out of "bottoms," with children voting on which one they liked the best.
- Talk about the consequences of Bear's actions and other consequences within the story.

LINEAR STORY DRAMA (BEFORE OR AFTER READING THE BOOK)

Caps for Sale
From the Esphyr Slobodkina version (or use your own)

This is a tale of a poor cap peddler whose only customers are a tree full of monkeys.

Materials Materials to make caps and monkey tails.

Introduction Talk about the capseller's work. Do they know how hats are made? Discuss other jobs with which the children are familiar.

Dramatization

- Make imaginary or real hats, gluing on feathers, flowers, beads, bells, or whatever they want. Caps can be made from newspapers, baseball caps that children are asked to bring from home, or paper plates, bent, with ribbons for ties. Count them.
- Set up a village, using chairs to represent houses or shops along a street. Place a card on each chair with the name and a

picture of the person who lives there or the type of store. Small groups of two or three children can live together or work together in a shop.

- Take on the role of capseller, taking a bag of hats (imaginary or real) to the villagers to sell. Encourage the villagers to come outside and try on the different hats. Perhaps an assistant can lead them in tossing off the hats (too big, too small, too feathery, etc.).
- Take time to develop monkey characters. Children can add on features with gestures or add a cloth tail.
- You may want to prepare for the next part of the story by practicing "mirroring" of each other's monkey gestures, first in a large circle, then in pairs.
- The monkeys could stand on a sturdy table, or outdoor climber, as they watch you fall asleep. When you awake to find the monkeys wearing your caps, add whatever motions you want and have the monkeys copy, finally throwing your cap down for them to follow.

Closing You will need a peaceful closing to calm their silliness after this drama. Parents could be invited as reporters to interview the cap peddlers (or monkeys) about their adventures.

Other Choices

- Bring bananas for children to taste to help them assume their monkey roles.
- Extend the drama to three days, focusing the first session on hat making, the second on setting up the homes or shops, and the third on the monkey scene.

ZOMO THE RABBIT
From the book by Gerald McDermott

This is a story about a clever rabbit who plays tricks on other animals, only to learn that the God of Wisdom has played a trick on him.

Introduction Begin by introducing children to the environment of West Africa. Possibilities: Look at a globe and talk about the journey from the United States to West Africa; focus on the heat of a tropical forest; use scarves as rain forest birds, butterflies, and snakes; construct a West African village and taste West African food—(sweet potatoes and coconut); or make drums and practice drumming different rhythms.

Dramatization Try to keep the playful spirit of this story by using a parachute as a colorful stage and involving a lot of pantomime and clever sound effects. Let small groups of children take turns acting out the different characters and scenarios while the rest manipulate the parachute to the rhythm of West African drumming and dance music. This group can function as the chorus.

- The chorus can use a lot of pantomime—Zomo climbing the tree, Zomo's chuckles as he tricks the animals, and the fish's horror at being caught naked.
- Shiny stickers can be used for the fish scales, with the "fish" swimming "underwater," then emerging through the center of the parachute to "shed their scales." The "cows" can use birthday hats as horns and can bellow and charge across the "forest floor"(parachute). As the "leopards" roll across the "forest floor," let others pop bubble wrap to create the sound of the "popping teeth." Perhaps every child could take a turn "running" in the parachute as Zomo, while the rest mime the Sky God's laughter and the other animals' furious roars.

Closing The children fold up the parachute and put away all of the props.

Other Choices
- Play a tape of tropical sounds.
- Let children create the sound effects with the pantomime— stones or clappers for charging cows, rattles for shimmying fish.
- Extend this drama to three days. Emphasize Zomo's desire to be all the things he isn't: strong, brave, wise. Then focus the second session on his cleverness: his ability to play tricks on fish, cow, and leopard. Finally, relate to the children, at an appropriate level, the Sky God's ability to show Zomo that "wisdom is more important than being smart."

EXTENDED STORY DRAMA

The Giant Jam Sandwich
From the book by Janet Burroway

This is a story about an English village afflicted with a plague of wasps. When commonplace measures fail, the villagers resort to making a giant jam sandwich to entrap the wasps.

Introduction Think of as many creative ways as you can to get to England (the setting of this story). This could be literal (such as taking a plane or boat) or more fanciful (on a cloud or tip-toeing over the rainbow).

Once you've arrived, think of interesting ways to introduce the British culture. Go to a tea party with the Queen, where they practice their manners.

Storytelling As you plan the storytelling for each session, think of ways the children can participate while sitting in the circle. Here are some suggestions:

- Develop a basic finger-play by wrapping pipe cleaners around their fingers to represent first wasps and then the harassed people. Let the children reshape the cleaners for each scene. Clothespins, with waxed paper for wings, also make good wasp puppets.
- You might also introduce either play dough or real bread dough into the story circle, giving each child the chance to feel, knead and shape their own "sandwich." Either way, raisins work well as "wasps" they can trap inside their sandwiches. Once the wasps are captured, children can become birds, eating the raisin-filled sandwiches (or miming the representational version).

Dramatization The most dramatic scene here is the four million wasps terrorizing the villagers. It's important to find ways to contain this improvisation, to give it distinct parameters. *The Flight of the Bumble Bee* makes great "wasp" music. Raise and lower the volume to control the speed and level of the "wasps'" movement. Pause the music at times and have the "wasps" freeze in wasplike positions.

- Choose distinctive costumes to turn children into wasps, such as pieces of waxed paper for wings, egg-box wasp eyes, or straw stingers. Agree with the children ahead of time on how you're going to act out "stinging." Emphasize that wasps don't sting each other.
- Making the huge loaf of bread can be enacted in a range of exciting ways: Bring in large down comforters for them to roll out as dough, or large pieces of paper that can be finger painted with all kinds of "jam" (pudding, paint, real jelly, if you choose). Older children can figure out the measurements of the ingredients to make the bread giant-sized.
- Capturing the wasps presents its own problem. Let children become the villagers and/or the birds who solve the problem

rather than become the wasps that are eaten. Represent wasps by using hand prints or raisins to stick to the "bread."

- When the sandwich is finished, use a whirligig to generate the sound and visual effect of a helicopter. Once the sandwich is made, children can become birds again and carry it out to sea.
- Let children dress up in costumes from the dress-up box to meet the Queen of England (you in role). The "villagers" then greet the Queen, remembering their manners, and tell her about the extraordinary event. Perhaps she can "knight" all the villagers with her royal scepter. Encourage the "villagers" to think of other suggestions for capturing the wasps.

Closing The Lords and Ladies sit at tables and make their own crowns out of paper, markers, and some adhesive "jewels." They can have a party to celebrate getting rid of the wasps. Find succinct ways to leave both the story and England behind and return home to school.

Other Choices

- Line up chairs in rows to create "a plane" and use squares of blue acetate as airplane windows. Spray the windows with a mister to create London fog when the plane lands.
- Make real bread, letting the children help you sift flour, mixing in salt and yeast.

Many of the suggestions in the full-length and abbreviated story dramas can be transferred to other stories. The possible adaptations and combinations are endless. As you begin to explore some of these strategies, you will discover what best suits your teaching style and your particular classroom dynamics. Once you are comfortable with using story dramatization, we hope you will consider the many other applications of drama presented in this book.

Notes

1. Though some of the stories in this book reflect various cultures and ethnicity, for a thorough description of using multiethnic material and several good examples, see Johnny Saldaña's book, *Drama of Color: Improvisation with Multiethnic Folklore.*

2. This format (one character meeting others along a journey somewhere or in search of something) fits many children's stories. Instead of meeting only one, the drama is adapted so that a few children represent each individual character. This format is also used in *Are You My Mother?* (Chapter 7).

3 ···

Beyond Story

The story dramas presented in Chapter 2 follow a fairly simple format, using the plot to guide the structure. Once teachers become comfortable using story drama in the classroom they may be hesitant to expand beyond these boundaries. Yet there are so many other kinds of learning experiences in the preschool and kindergarten classroom that can be initiated or enhanced through drama, it is worth taking the leap. This chapter explores ways of moving beyond the safe structure of a story drama.

We are using the term *theme-based drama* to describe drama work that does not originate from or in a story. Though stories generally follow a particular theme (and theme-based drama can evolve into a scenario or story), theme-based drama usually evolves from children's interests. To further clarify the four-way continuum of dramatic activity as described in Chapter 1, the following theme-based examples are separated into similar categories: incidental drama, evolving drama, and preplanned drama. Like all the other dramas detailed in this book, these drama sessions and extended dramas are one of a kind. Any material you adapt for your classes will assume a unique character based on the creative life and direction you and your students bring to it.

Incidental Drama

The two dramatic play episodes described here were introduced as spontaneous responses to children's play. In both scenarios, the teacher had no agenda other than to respond to and develop the content of what she observed. It is, however, possible to intervene with a specific objective and direction in mind, as illustrated in "Superhero Alert," which appears later in the chapter.

"PREPARING FOR WINTER" [3]

Dramatic Play Scenario This drama work initially came from a few children playing with plastic animal toys. The tigers and lions were fighting

with the bears, and one child decided that the bears could get away by
going to the cave to "hidanate."

LUCUS: I'm gonna go "hidanate" in my cave and that means you can't get me
there cause I'm sleepin'. (*Lucus makes a quick cave with some curved blocks.*)
ANNAD: I can go in the back way.
LUCAS: No. The lions are afraid to wake up the bear in his cave. Don't do that.
TERRY: Then we get a cave, too.
ANNAD: Lions don't sleep in caves, they sleep on big rocks and growl if
you get on their rock. (*He makes a loud growling sound and Terry joins in
with his lion growling along.*)

On the playground that afternoon, there were several children pretending to be bears and looking for caves in which to hide. They took
turns being the lion that chased the bears, who were safe under the
climber–bear cave.

Drama When the children come in from the playground, the teacher
spends a good amount of time exploring "bear movement." She encourages the bears to search for berries and other bear food from the forest
because it is almost time for hibernation.

Closing Through drama, they explore the concept of hibernation by
finding a cave under a table and are each wrapped up in a sleeping bag to
stay warm until spring time. This ritual of searching for food to "fatten
up" for winter and then curling up in a warm cave is repeated several
times by the children in their own play. Eventually the teacher introduces
other animals' winter habits.

"THE PT BIRDS AND THE SAND CREATURES"

Dramatic Play Scenario The teacher had observed the children playing outside in two groups—five in the sandbox and three underneath the
slide. He wanted to develop the scope of the children's play without
breaking their focus.

Drama—Part One The teacher gathers children into a circle and asks
them to talk about their play. Children in the sandbox say they're making food for their children. "Are you people?" the teacher asks, "or animals?" "Animals," one of the more dominant children replies, with the
result that the rest of the group concurs that they are all indeed animals.
The teacher decides to go along with this, rather than encourage more
individuation at this juncture. "What kind of animals?" he asks." "Sand
Creatures," a second child says. "What are you Justin?" he asks one of
the quieter children, who immediately says, "A Sand Creature." "What

does your Sand Creature look like?" the teacher asks, deciding to go with the flow. After some deliberation, Justin says he's purple and furry with floppy ears. The teacher encourages each child to come up with their own colors and features and to resist imitation. He writes down these descriptions.

The teacher then repeats this exercise with the "slide children," who identify themselves as the PT Birds (because they say "peetee, peetee, peetee"), living in a deep, dark cave. *The dominant child in this group tries to steer the group toward being "Batmans," but the teacher resists, using the logic that it would be more fun if each group was a different kind of animal because then they could later become scientists, do research, and learn a lot of new stuff about these animal species.* By now, the group is getting restless, so the teacher sends them back to their play areas to explore being Sand Creatures and PT Birds.

Drama—Part Two While they're playing, the teacher comes around and asks more exploratory questions about what the animals eat, how they move, where they sleep, how many young they have, if they're born or laid as eggs (the teacher suggests that birds tend to lay eggs), whether they're nocturnal or diurnal, and so on. Some of these questions work to direct the drama. For example, when he asks about the young, one of the PT Birds introduces a crate as an egg and sits on it. The other two PT Birds immediately do the same and a long "hatching" routine ensues.

Drama—Part Three After about another ten minutes, the play is visibly winding down; one of the PT Birds has left the game because he wants to feed his own baby and not participate in the communal feeding ritual the other two prefer. The teacher brings out a spray bottle, spraying everyone with "rain." It's time to wash off their animal selves, become children again, and get inside before the "rain" gets any harder.

Drama—Part Four Once back in the classroom, the teacher turns the children into scientists by having them put on protective clothing (art aprons) to prepare reports on the new animal species they've just discovered. Each child makes a "picture report" of one or both animals and the teacher takes dictation. He reminds several children of details that came up during the drama, so they can include them in the reports if they want to. Some want their pictures hung up separately as photographic reports.

Follow-up Later on, the teacher decides to create a narrative about the two groups in order to encourage the two to interact. A long drama ensues where the two groups "go to war"; the Sand Creatures steal an egg from the PTs' nest but, with some coaxing from the teacher, they fall in love with the baby chick (as opposed to eating her), and eventually resolve to give her back to her parents.

Evolving Drama

These theme-based dramas were child initiated and developed in response to children's interest and involvement. The first, "Space Travel," though more linear and narrative in structure, evolved not only in response to children's fascination with space, but also to their ongoing input—it's the children who decide to visit the moon and on the kinds of space gear they want to make. The teacher's creative responses are designed either to implement the children's ideas, perpetuate the narrative (the dust storm), or deepen children's reflection (the letter to moon visitors).

"The Hospital" falls under the heading of improvisational structures devised to enlarge and extend themes already expressed in the children's play. Once these basic systems—the various areas of the hospital or restaurant—are set up, they generate ongoing improvisation. The teacher's role here is to maintain momentum. Through questioning and modeling, children's work becomes richer, particularly their use of language.

"Space Travel"

Objective To broaden the children's curiosity and awareness of the sun, moon, and stars and to increase awareness of distance (close, far away, and very far away).

Beginning The drama was initiated by children building a rocket ship together in the large block area of a preschool classroom. They wanted to keep their project up for several days, adding cardboard boxes and painting on a control board. This motivated others to join in the play and generated lots of discussion about outer space. The scenario that evolved is a journey into outer space, including a visit to the moon.

Drama Following is a summary of the progression of events for this ten-session drama work that evolved out of the children's curiosity and interests. The work goes back and forth between free play and teacher-directed drama. For this reason, we have chosen not to break it down into daily sessions.

- The teacher spreads out a parachute (a large sheet would do) and has the children take hold of the outside. She then fills it with neon confetti and dims the lights. She plays "astral" music (such as excerpts from Gustav Holtz's *The Planets Suite*) and directs children to "shake up the stars." She tells the children they are looking deep into space at all the suns and planets in the cosmos. They put the parachute down and collect some glitter. Then they go to tables, where they make a picture with chalk and dark-colored construction paper of their planet and its surrounding moons, gluing on the glitter they've collected.

- Children look at pictures of astronauts and spaceships and discuss why the astronauts have to wear special suits and use oxygen tanks. They decide that they will have to have oxygen tanks for their journey into outer space, and make a list of other things they will need, such as special food and water bottles. They debate how many water bottles they will need to take for the length of time they will be in space and how their bodies will be lighter; they practice "walking in space."

- Children make oxygen masks from empty plastic milk cartons, making straps to wear like backpacks. Anxious to "blast off," they decide to take a short practice flight and walk in space before their big trip to the moon. The potentially frenzied action of "blasting off" is all done in place, with children leaning back against upside down chairs. They travel thousands of miles without moving from their spot.

- In order to travel through space, they use a long rope, connected to their space ship, as a safety cable. Children must hold onto the rope with one hand while they "fly through space." When they return, they describe what they have seen on their imaginary journey. Follow-up includes making "space rocks" in clay and painting them with wild designs and colors.

- After several days, the room has been decorated with a space map, all sorts of stars hanging from the ceiling, planets, and a big picture of the moon. The teacher has collected a variety of things, which children will use to collect rocks and unusual things from the moon's surface. Children practice picking up small blocks and putting them in a plastic "gathering" bag. They create a checklist for their journey and write a letter that they will leave on the moon, inviting whoever finds it to visit them on earth.

- All children strap themselves into their rocket ship seats (as before) and begin the countdown. As they travel to the moon, the teacher turns off the lights, darkening the room, and plays the previous astral music. She sets the parachute out as the moon's surface, adding the moon rocks. As the song ends, she narrates a description of the approaching moon, ending with, "Looks like we've landed safely!" Children slowly open their "doors" and step onto the moon. They are reminded about moving slowly as they search for and collect moon rocks. The teacher announces that there is a dust storm coming and they must get back to their ship. They get in the ship (a circle created by the upside down chairs) as the moon dust covers them up. They will go to sleep inside the ship and continue their journey in the morning.

- This session begins with the children inside their ship, the morning after the moon dust storm. The teacher passes around moon dust (corn meal) for them to feel. They "wake up" to a breakfast of juice from their water bottle and Cheerios in a plastic bag (so they won't float away). A discussion evolves about solutions for getting rid of the moon dust covering up their entrance. Suggestions include rocking the ship until the dust falls off, waiting for a wind storm to blow it off, and using their special blower guns to blow it away. After trying a couple of these ideas, they continue their search and find a good place to leave their letter.

- On the seventh day of this extended drama, the children get back in their spaceship and return to earth. They touch down in water and must get on a ship and sail back to land (with wobbly legs). Parents have been invited to join the class in the role of newspaper reporters. The reporters and astronauts have a welcome-home celebration, parents throwing streamers as the astronauts come off of the boat and taking photos of the proud astronauts. After a snack, the reporters gather children in groups of two or three and interview them about their space adventure. They take notes, which become part of a newspaper the children are creating with drawings and photographs of their experience.

- A week later, children are taken to the playground to discover pieces of painted board and odd-shaped knobs and things (preset). They bring the strange pieces back to the classroom and put them together to create a small spaceship. The note they had left on the moon is also there. There is a great deal of discussion about who might have traveled in the ship and where they might have gone. They decide that if the visitor shows up, they will be prepared to share some things about their world. They are asked to bring a favorite toy, game, stuffed animal, or food the following day.

- A friend of the teacher takes on the role of the visiting alien (wearing an oddly decorated cap to distinguish him from earthlings), sitting inside the spaceship for the children to discover when they return from the playground. The children are delighted, but the alien does not speak the same language, so they must use gestures. The teacher divides them into four groups: toys, games, animals, and foods. The alien goes around to each group, learning about these things from earth.

- The following day, the children learn that their visitor doesn't know about the five senses (a subject they have been talking a lot about). They decide to set up a "Five Sense" center and are asked to bring from home something to smell, taste, touch, see, and hear. The next day the alien returns, visiting each of the five tables, where groups of children teach him about the five senses. He selects one item from each table to take back to his planet.

Closing After a ceremonial parting, with photos, children have lots to write and draw about in their "newspaper journals."

"THE HOSPITAL"

Materials White crepe streamers (bandages), Q-tips (syringes), M & Ms (pills), blankets, trays (for wards), surgical gloves, pollen masks, goggles, various pieces of tubing (surgery gear), clipboards (intake), a siren, hats, and a wheelchair (ambulance).

Objective To help children overcome their fear of hospitals by acting out a number of the "power" roles themselves and to practice team-building and cooperative skills.

Beginning This one-day event grew out of the children's dramatic play and their preoccupation with doctors and nurses. One child had been taken from the playground by ambulance after falling and breaking her arm. The teacher wanted to extend this to involve the whole class and give them the experience of participating and sustaining an extended large-scale activity.

Drama The teacher begins by introducing a surgical (pollen) mask, and after letting children feel its unusual surface, she puts it over her face. "Who might wear a mask like this?" she asks. "A doctor," Jose, one of the children involved in hospital play, replies. "Okay," the teacher says, "now you put it over your face and show me with your body what kinds of jobs a doctor does." The other children "read" Jose's actions, and then take turns acting out other hospital roles, including nurse and anesthesiologist. The teacher interjects some vocabulary herself, to distinguish the difference between the surgeon and the physician. "Why do these people wear masks?" the teacher asks next. "It keeps the dirt and flies out," one child says. The teacher then asks if they know what other kinds of jobs there are in a hospital; the list grows to include ambulance drivers and in-take clerks. Next, the teacher asks the class to come up with a list of different conditions and illnesses that bring people to the hospital.

- The teacher reads the list of roles and, together with the children, decides the different areas of the hospital each group belongs in. Children then pick a role while the teacher makes sure the numbers add up to a viable system (two surgeons, one anesthesiologist, two physicians, five nurses, two ambulance drivers, one intake clerk, seven patients). Everyone will eventually have a chance to play every role.

- The teacher has brought in four boxes of props but is open to the children's suggestions and innovations. One box is for the ward, another for surgery, the third for the intake desk and the emergency room, and the fourth for the ambulance. Each group sets up its area, with the patients divided up among all four.

- Once the action begins, the teacher's role is to keep it moving. If there's a backup in intake, the teacher can become or appoint a second clerk to move things along.

- After ten minutes or so, the teacher freezes the action and switches some of the recovered patients with the surgery staff, some nurses with the ambulance drivers. In this way, she injects new enthusiasm and energy into the action; fifteen minutes later, she switches the children's roles again. In doing so, children stay engaged for forty minutes.

- At the children's suggestion, this scenario is reconstructed later in the semester, only this time the hospital is a veterinary clinic, inspired by their play and discussion of their pets and stuffed animals.

Preplanned Drama

These teacher-initiated, theme-based dramas were outlined in advance to address specific curricular goals. The village scenario in "The Stranger," could easily have evolved out of the children's play. It was, in this instance, a premeditated ploy on the part of a teacher looking for an age-appropriate way to address homelessness with her class. (There was a weekly soup kitchen held in the same building as the school and some children were expressing curiosity.) Similarly, "Your Own Back Yard" is intended to heighten children's awareness of urban pollution. "The Trip to the Beach" was developed specifically for children with no prior experience of the ocean. Nonetheless, all the drama sessions allow room for flexibility and child initiative, both within individual dramatic activities as well as in the pace and direction of the overall sequence.

"THE STRANGER"

Objective To encourage sympathy and caring feelings towards others and to engage in problem-solving strategies.

Beginning The teacher chose to introduce the stranger into a dramatic environment (the village) rather than directly into the classroom. Her reasoning was that, through the drama, children would be problem solving within an imaginary context rather than practicing real-life (potentially risky) behaviors they might repeat with strangers in the street.

Scenario Children in the role of villagers, faced with the decision of rejecting or caring for a homeless stranger.

DAY ONE: CONSTRUCTING THE VILLAGE

Materials Large cardboard boxes (one per child is best, but fewer will work) and painting supplies.

Introduction During circle time, the teacher brings in a large pile of cardboard boxes and tells the class they're going to use them to make houses.

Construction The children are very excited about choosing their own boxes and tell the teachers where to cut off flaps, cut out windows and add in chimneys. They quickly start painting, choosing colors and designs for their own homes. Several girls decide to build a group house; a while later, another decides she would prefer to join the group house rather than continue living in her single dwelling. The teacher suggests she put her house up for sale. She makes a sign, and one of the boys buys her house.

Drama The children share their "homes" well, although they clearly feel pride of ownership and want to be asked permission and to grant it before visiting one another's houses. Snack time is integrated into the improvisation, and some choose to picnic outside, while others share a meal indoors. Others choose to eat in the privacy of their own homes.

Closing "Night" comes (the blinds are drawn) and the children all fall asleep in their homes. When they wake up, it's time to clean up the boxes and go outside, where some of the dramatic scenarios carry over into outdoor play.

Follow-up The children make a map of the village, including color, shape, and inhabitants' names.

DAY TWO: DEVELOPING COMMUNITY

Materials A large sheet of cardboard or paper to write on and markers.

Introduction During circle time, the children develop a constitution for their village. There is great consistency to the discussion: privacy, permission, hurting, noise, and mess control.

Village Constitution:
1. You are supposed to live in your own house.
2. No fighting and killing in our village. No wrestling. No hurting.
3. If somebody wants to be alone in their house, that can be so. Someone can ask to come in your house.
4. If you make a mess in our village, you have to clean it up. We don't want to mess our village up.
5. You have to take care of each other's houses.
6. The village should be nice and quiet.
7. Don't throw trash on the floors, and don't be goofy!

Drama The teacher decides to continue the village improvisation to see how it develops. A group of boys gets involved in taking care of babies (dolls from the playhouse). They spend a lot of time figuring out family roles and responsibilities (e.g., who's the father and who's the neighbor). Whenever one particular father goes out, he asks another to watch his baby for him.

DAY THREE (PART ONE): DEFINING ROLES

Materials Simple costumes and props to help dramatize the villagers' jobs.

Introduction During circle time, children pick jobs. Many choose multiple roles. One boy chooses Daddy and Baker, another girl is an Artist, Mummy, and Doctor.

Drama As the children play, they pick out props to match their roles (e.g., the baker makes "muffins" (blocks) and "sells them" from his house). On the third day, it is much easier for the children to share their houses and move in and out of one another's lives. The teacher feels the children's commitment to their imaginary community is such that this is the right moment to introduce the stranger.

DAY THREE (PART TWO): MEETING THE STRANGER

Materials Ice, lemon juice, dirt, a costume for Emma, and a letter.

Introduction After lunch, the teacher brings in some costume pieces— a sweater, a hat, and a purse—and tells the children they belong to her friend, "Emma." She describes Emma as suffering from a bad cold and a sore back and mimes both ailments. She then explains how cold Emma gets because she lives outside, and then passes an ice cube around the circle so children can experience what Emma feels. The teacher tells them how hungry Emma gets because she doesn't get enough to eat, and then she gives them each a taste of Emma's hunger (lemon juice). Finally, she explains how dirty Emma gets because she doesn't have anywhere to wash her clothes or herself, and then rubs a little dirt in the children's palms.

The teacher explains that Emma is going to visit the village while the villagers are asleep, and directs the children to become the sleeping villagers.

Drama While the villagers are asleep (the blinds are drawn), Emma (the teacher in costume) approaches the village, complaining about how cold and hungry she is and how badly her back is hurting. When she notices the houses, she remarks on their different colors and features, how beautiful they all are. She says how very much she would like a home of her own. Several of the children want to get up and come out of their houses, but the aide reminds them that it's nighttime and the villagers are asleep in their beds.

After Emma leaves the room, the aide announces that morning has come (opens the blinds) and immediately calls a village meeting. (You could actually remove your costume, and return to guide the discussion.) She asks the villagers what they heard and saw in the night. Some identify Emma, while a couple say a monster came. Several repeat things Emma said. The aide asks if any of them were frightened by Emma, and one boy says, "Yes"; she takes time to acknowledge his feelings by saying that hearing people moving about outside in the night can indeed be frightening, though usually they don't mean any harm. She adds, "If you hear people outside your house at night, you should get up and tell your parents."

The aide then produces a letter that Emma "dropped" on the ground. It says:

Dear Emma,
You have not paid your rent, so you will have to lose your
house.
The City Council

Sitting in the circle, they close their eyes and go back in time to imagine what Emma's house might have looked like. They mention different colors, a garden, toys, a car, and a washing machine. They go to the tables and draw pictures of their own versions of Emma's old house.

Back in the circle, several children volunteer to share their houses with Emma, while others feel threatened. (Those who do feel threatened witness the generosity of others, while the "overgenerous" must face the consequences of their own altruistic impulses—there's only so much living space in one house, and besides, the stranger may not want to accept their invitation.) One girl pipes up that she would like to build Emma a house of her own, and everyone agrees. An extra box is brought into the circle and everyone sets about decorating and furnishing it. One girl is adamant about installing a bath and setting out some soap. The aide asks how the children plan to let Emma know that the house is hers, and they suggest writing a note with Emma's name on it and pinning it to the roof.

At nightfall the villagers go to sleep and Emma returns and is delighted to discover her new home. The villagers burst out of their houses to help her move in.

Closing The aide calls the children back to the circle, and the teacher slowly removes her costume and changes her posture and voice. She praises the children for treating Emma so well and explains that it's now time for her to stop pretending to be Emma and for them to stop pretending to be villagers. At the end of the day, the children take their houses home.

Follow-up The teacher notices that the children ask about Emma for several days after the drama and decides to bring in Emma's purse so they can learn more about her life from its contents. There are pictures of pets, as well as a grocery list and some train tickets. The teacher decides to leave Emma single and childless, but wonders what the consequences would be of giving her a family.

The teacher also notices that several of these prekindergartners have been able to articulate concerns about classroom dynamics in the context of the village (e.g., noise level and messiness) that they haven't felt comfortable bringing up before. After the drama, however, these children express themselves more freely during circle time.

"YOUR OWN BACK YARD"

Objective To demonstrate an awareness of the effect pollution has on the environment and employ related problem-solving strategies.

Beginning The scenario of this drama developed from what children had already been studying: their neighborhood, including the animals they were familiar with (birds, squirrels, and cats). The problem was one with which the children were familiar: people in a crowded neighborhood, dumping trash and garbage in the park, and air polluted by too many cars. In the role of the animals being affected by the pollution, the children experience and explore the consequences of pollution.

DAY ONE

Materials A letter from Ali Cat, realistic pictures of squirrels and birds, and pictures depicting pollution.

Introduction The teacher gathers the children into a circle to share the fictitious letter she's received from Ali Cat:

> Dear Boys and Girls,
> My name is Ali and I live in a park, but that is okay because I am a cat. There are also birds and squirrels that live in this park. We used to be very happy here. Now we have a problem. Our park is becoming polluted. We heard that you are studying pollution. We also heard that you know a lot about drama. I would like to come to your school and talk to you. Maybe we can use drama to find a solution to the pollution.
> Sincerely,
> Ali Cat

The children have many questions about the situation. After a good discussion, they decide they would take on the roles of the birds and squirrels in the drama.

Drama The teacher shows the children pictures of squirrels. They discuss their distinctive features, using hand shapes to add these features onto their bodies, like costume pieces (little squirrel ears, big brown eyes, wiggly nose, long front teeth, and long bushy tail). They practice squirrel movements, running quickly, stopping and looking all around, and so forth. They are searching for imaginary acorns. The teacher switches the lights on and off as a sign to the squirrels to stop and look for danger. This works nicely to control the movement. Finally they return to the circle to bury their acorns.

- A similar routine transforms the children into birds. They rub off their squirrel fur as the teacher shows them several bird pictures, including some exotic colorful birds. "Which of these birds might live in a city park?" she asks. Using gestures, they create their bird costumes by adding on their beaks, little eyes, bird toes, and long bird wings. After some practice flying around the room, they gather together to discuss bird diets. Using the lights again as a control mechanism, they are sent around the room to collect worms or seeds. They return to feed baby birds in a nest.

Closing Children ask if they can become baby birds, so the teacher has all her "baby birds" snuggle close together in the imaginary nest. As she mimes giving each a worm or seed, she encourages them to fall asleep in the nest. When the wiggling dies down, she uses a feather duster to brush the bird costumes off the sleeping birds.

Follow-up Children are still excited about meeting the cat. The teacher sets up an art activity to help focus their energy. Most paint pictures of a squirrel and/or bird. Some add a cat.

Day Two

Materials A large handmade map of the setting (park and surrounding buildings) and perhaps a tail and headband-ears for the teacher's cat costume.

Introduction The teacher demonstrates how she will become Ali Cat using the headband-ears and tail. The children want the teacher to go outside of the classroom to put on her cat costume and knock on the door. This works nicely, with Ali Cat asking if she has the right classroom and showing amazement at their beautiful school (no pollution!). After an impromptu tour of the class, they gather in a circle to hear her story. (If you are not comfortable portraying Ali Cat, a cat puppet or stuffed animal can be effective. An outside teacher or actor might visit the class as Ali Cat, though this is not as logistically workable as the first two options.)

Drama Ali Cat's narrative begins: "I'm so glad to be here. Your school is so nice and clean, green grass and trees all around, and the air outside is so fresh. It reminds me of the park I live in—I mean the way it used to be. When I was a young cat, we had lots of trees, grass, and flowers all around. The air was fresh, and I used to play with the birds and squirrels all day." They try to imagine what games a cat might play with birds and squirrels; maybe tag (since cats chase birds) and maybe hide-and-seek. Ali Cat agrees and describes how she was always "it": "The birds and squirrels would all sit in one tree, and I would slowly climb up the tree to try to catch one. Just as I got to the top, they would all fly, or hop over to the next tree. Would you like to try this game?"

Children divide into two groups: birds and squirrels. The teacher switches back to her teacher role, helping children with this transition. Returning to her Ali Cat role, she takes the children back in time "when the park was clean and green." They imagine where the gardens would be and set up chairs in the room to represent the trees. They gather around a tree in groups of four or five birds or squirrels. As Ali pretends to slowly climb up the "tree," they fly or hop to another, empty tree. This is great fun for the children, each group getting at least two turns to fly or hop away.

Back to the circle. Ali thanks the children for helping her remember how much fun it used to be in her park and then says, "Now there are no more games. Most of us feel sick from the pollution, and it is dangerous to run around because there is a lot of broken glass and old cans with sharp edges." (She licks her paw, remembering an old injury.) Children agree to help Ali find a way to stop the humans from polluting the park. Some suggest taking a bus to the park to help her, but she convinces them it is too far away.

Closing The children use the feather duster again to dust off their imaginary costumes. Then they listen and sing along to a song called "Living Planet" (by Jay Mankita on a tape or CD by Magpie called "Living Planet," and sung by Terry Leonino and Greg Artzner). (There are other age-appropriate songs on this tape, and another by Magpie, called "Circle of Life," that relate to caring for the planet.)

Follow-up The children begin work on a big mural of the park, to help Ali remember how beautiful it once was. This becomes a week-long project.

DAY THREE

Materials Pictures of pollution, a flower, a pack of flower seeds, and blocks or other props to represent the trash.

Introduction A few days have passed since the last drama session, but the children have been working daily on their park mural for Ali. They gather into the circle and review the different types of pollution, looking at pictures.

Drama The teacher, changing into costume in the hall as requested, returns as Ali Cat, coughing. She is getting sicker from the air pollution in her park: "Now, the eggs that the birds have laid are not hatching and acorns that the squirrels buried last fall cannot be found under all the trash. Everyone is hungry, but the plants are not safe to eat. My friends sent this with me to give you (she hands them a somewhat wilted flower)—the last flower to grow in our park."

- To engage all the children in the problem-solving task, the class is divided into groups of three to four children (teacher and assistant going between the groups to facilitate discussion). One group suggests that the animals can move to their school and live. Another proposes the squirrels bite the tires of the cars "so they can't go anymore and won't make pollution." This invites discussion about damaging property, but Ali suggests it might be a way of getting the people to take the bus or walk instead, which would be a good thing. The class particularly likes one group's plan to carry the trash from the park to the front doors of the houses, "so people can see what it feels like to live with garbage." They will also deliver the nest of "sick eggs," so people will know the pollution is hurting animals.

- They create the polluted park by scattering classroom blocks around the space. Chairs represent cars, and tables represent the surrounding houses. Ali helps children transform into birds and squirrels again. The lights are turned out and shades pulled down to create "nighttime." It doesn't take long for the children to carry out their plan, pretending to bite car tires and pushing the block-trash to the front doors of imaginary buildings.
- Back to the circle. Ali asks if they would like to pretend to be the people that live in the buildings. They quickly brush away their bird or squirrel costumes, eagerly select a home at one of the tables (two to three children per table), and pretend to be sleeping. As morning arrives (lights and curtains up), they are extremely animated when discovering the trash and flat tires.
- The teacher now takes on the role of a neighbor and calls a neighborhood meeting to discuss what they have found. Everyone is talking at once, even some of the most shy children in the class. They agree to clean up the park for the animals and promise to walk to work or take the bus.

Closing The teacher switches back to Ali Cat. She can't wait to return to her friends and share the children's ideas. Children show Ali the park mural they have created. She promises to let them know how things work out. They all sit in a circle again and review the "Living Planet" song.

Discussion Children have said good-bye to Ali (with lots of hugs). The teacher reminds the children that it may take a long time to clean up the pollution and make the park look beautiful again. They agree that, in their next drama, they will pretend it is a year later and see what has happened to the park. They write a letter to Ali Cat to wish her good luck, send her a pack of flower seeds, and invite her back "one year from now."

DAY FOUR

Materials Photos of a park with trees and flowers, and stickers of squirrels (or cats).

Introduction Though it has only been a few days since the last drama sessions, the children agree that "in drama time" it is one year later. It is their idea to have a party with Ali. They decorate cookies with cat ears and whiskers and discuss possible party games, agreeing to play tag and hide-and-seek with Ali again.

Drama The teacher leaves and returns as Ali Cat for one last visit. They gather around her as she shares the story of what happened with their plan (exactly as they had predicted in their dramatization). "The people created a 'Green and Clean' day for the park, clearing away all the trash and planting your flower seeds. They built a beautiful bird feeder (the squirrels sometimes climb up and eat from it, too). The park looks just like your mural."

The party: Ali helps the children create the park again, setting up chairs in the room to represent the trees. They repeat the game playing from the earlier session, including hide-and-seek, with the squirrels and birds finding a hiding place while Ali counts to ten. They must fly or hop back to the circle when she spots them.

Closing All gather at the tables for cat-cookies with Ali, listening to earth-friendly music as they eat. Ali thanks the children and places a sticker of a bird or squirrel on the back of each child's hand to help them remember, then says good-bye.

Discussion Children review the series of events and talk about what little things children can do to prevent pollution. They discuss recycling and other ideas they have learned over the last two weeks.

Follow-up A bird, squirrel, and cat puppet and some plastic miniatures are left in the dramatic play area for the children to integrate into their dramatic play. Small recycling bins are also added to the kitchen play area.

Special Needs Separating into two groups (birds and squirrels) is difficult for some children. Hanging pictures of a child's animal around his neck helps him to remember which animal group he is in as well as identify his classmates' characters. In this class, there was one child with cerebral palsy who could not participate in the tag game. He was given a can and a stick to warn the birds and squirrels when the cat was getting too close.

Suggestions for More Theme-based Drama

The following theme-based dramas are presented in abbreviated form to spark your creativity and imagination. They were selected due to the common nature of the themes and are presented in a directive format to suggest how you might develop this type of work. Your choices, of course, will be guided by your children's specific responses. (For example, instead of entering the stomach of a whale, they may come up with the idea of riding in a submarine!)

INCIDENTAL DRAMA

"SUPERHERO ALERT!"

Dramatic Play Scenario Young children can become absorbed in play related to their favorite cartoon super heroes. Though action figures are usually not permitted in early childhood settings, this fascination often influences their dramatic play.[1] This scenario began with children creating guns from blocks and Tinker Toys, and "blasting away the bad guys." Rather than banning this kind of play in the classroom, consider a drama intervention to redirect the scenario. The objective is to stimulate more imaginative thinking and encourage children to come up with nonviolent solutions to aggression.

Drama Enter the play with a "Hero Hat" (a souped-up version of a motorcycle helmet), delivering an emergency message from Hero Headquarters. All superheroes have an important new task: They must stop fighting the bad guys with guns. Instead, they must invent new weapons that can capture the enemy alive. If children ask why, explain that we're running out of bad guys to fight, or the mommies of the bad guys are growing sad.

- Gather suggestions from children in an "Emergency Superhero Meeting," creating a written list of their ideas. Children have come up with suggestions such as a tickle gun, which tickles the bad guys so badly they fall over; shoe glue, which you spray on their feet to make them stick to the ground; and an ice cube blaster, which freezes the enemy in place.
- Once you have three or four fairly nonviolent suggestions, divide children into "invention teams" to create drawings of what their ideas will look like. These can also be models made with clay, Tinker Toys, pipe cleaners, paper towel tubes, and so on.
- Create a demonstration day, when the inventors present their new creations to Superhero Headquarters by dramatizing short "capturing scenarios."

Closing Discuss what they might do with the "bad guys" once they are caught. Answers from children have included, "They can be on our team as long as they don't hurt us," and "stay frozen for ten years until they forget how to be bad." Draw pictures of superheroes and bad guys with "thought bubbles," writing in children's suggestions for their character's thoughts.

EVOLVING DRAMA

"THE RESTAURANT" [3]

Objective To practice working in a large group and to create a scenario to discuss nutrition, numeration, and different food traditions.

Beginning Cooking and food production is a popular subject for children's play. To expand this dramatic play for a full classroom drama, begin by writing a menu—also a good opportunity to discuss food groups and general nutrition. The teacher can encourage children from different ethnic backgrounds to talk about the food they eat at home. Pass around some condiments, herbs, and spices to smell and taste.

Drama Children can spend time creating the foods to be served in their restaurant with clay, construction paper, crayons, and scissors. White yarn works for spaghetti and colored yarn for sauce.

- The next step is to allocate roles: waiters, chefs, maitre d', cashier, and customers. Props and costume pieces define both role and activity.
- Once the restaurant is open and the action has begun, you may need to intervene to keep things going, and, if you feel so inclined, set up a problem situation such as a customer being unable to pay for a meal, swallowing a fish bone, or the kitchen running out of spaghetti.

Closing Close up the restaurant for the night and send everyone home. As they are driving home in their imaginary cars, run through a quick review of the "evening's" events.[2]

PREPLANNED DRAMA

"A Trip to the Beach"

Objective To introduce the experience of the ocean to children who have never been, and to deepen and enrich the knowledge base of those who have.

Beginning Initiate the theme with a large conch shell, which the children can feel and listen to as well as look at. Discuss what kind of creature might have lived inside, the age of the shell, and who might have taken it from the sea. Let each child hear the ocean "whispering," calling her to visit.

Day One Create "suitcases" out of paper napkins and mime filling them with everything necessary for the beach, then "close" (fold) and "zip" them (mime and make zipping sounds).

Board the school bus (rows of chairs), with the teacher in role as the driver, and drive down the highway to the beach. Have the bus break down and encourage the children to get out their tool kits (a box of straws), wriggle underneath the engine, and put things right. A straw can pass as any tool you like, including a gas nozzle or a portable phone! Reboard the bus and play an ocean tape, softly, at first and then more loudly as the bus gets closer to the "water." At "the beach," put on "sun block" (hand lotion) and spread out "towels" (the same paper napkins as were used for the suitcases). Make paper towels into surf boards and improvise a surf-boarding exercise. Children then rest on the beach while watching the red sun go down (flashlight shone through a piece of red acetate).

Day Two This time let the children choose their own modes of transportation to get to the beach. Use a long piece of blue cloth to create ocean waves, and salty water inside a spray bottle to create ocean water for the children to taste. Look at pictures of shorelife species such as crabs, lobsters, seaweed, and sea urchins. Pass out surgical gloves for the children to improvise their own versions. They can be worn to create crabs venturing out onto the sand then running for shelter under a rock (crossed legs) whenever a wave comes along, or the gloves can be removed and tweaked to make "squeaky seaweed." Blow into them and you have blow fish. Later, the children go swimming on a sheet or parachute, and the teacher can portray a lifeguard directing each "swimmer" in and out of the water. Afterwards, the swimmers rinse off in the shower (spray bottle).

Day Three Look at pictures of whales and dolphins and listen to tapes of their calls. Use a dab of oil to transform the children into slippery dolphins who take turns "swimming" and "jumping" in the "ocean" (parachute or large sheet). You might billow the parachute or sheet and sit underneath to create the "inside the belly of a giant whale." Solicit suggestions as to how you might all get out. Acknowledge the more violent ones, but act on the benign ones, such as tickling or talking to the whale.

Afterward, turn the empty parachute into a beached whale, which the children can measure for length and width. Find ways to help "the whale" get back into the water.

Closing Use the multisensory props like the paper napkins and the spray bottle to wipe and wash off the drama and restore the everyday world. While children are "asleep" on the beach, narrate trips back to school, reiterating all the elements of the previous session.

Day Four Turn children into deep sea divers with snorkels (straws) and underwater glasses (acetate squares), which they later use as underwater cameras to take photos of deep-sea life. "Develop" the photos later in an art project.

Follow-up Get children involved in other kinds of imaginary trips— Down the Amazon and into the Rain Forest, through caves, up a mountain. Allow room for problem solving—run out of food and water, meet a wild animal, have someone (better a teacher) get injured.

Integrating an Audience

No matter how adorable the children may seem in their drama work, resist the urge to create a performance. If you would like to have other teachers or parents see how successful their work in drama has been, consider integrating outsiders into the drama conclusion. Instead of putting on an end-of-year performance, give the parents the role of reporters or a TV crew, coming to interview the returning astronauts or take an account of the mysterious Sand Creatures, or turn the classroom into a spaghetti restaurant and dress the parents up as customers. If the classroom environment is "the hospital," the parents could become the patients. Even with a drama based on performance, such as a circus, the parents can just as easily be in the role of new circus trainees coming to learn from the professionals, instead of being audience members. Either situation puts the children in charge and therefore at ease, countering a tendency of young children to freeze up in performance. The children have very distinct roles and tasks—the waiters have to deliver the menus, take down orders, and deliver the food—which again dilutes self-consciousness. Scenarios like this rely on team effort and group cooperation, giving children an opportunity to interact with adults, with plenty of support from their peers. Again, the improvisational character of the event leaves room for more performance-oriented children to seize cameo moments without upstaging everyone else in the cast.

Notes

1. See Nancy Carlsson-Paige and Diane E. Levin's *Who's Calling the Shots?: How to Respond Effectively to Children's Fascination with War Play and War Toys,* and D. Levin's, *Teaching Children in Violent Times,* for an in-depth look at this issue. It has a wealth of suggestions for guiding children away from TV-generated and -stifled war play into more imaginative, enriching dramatic play.

2. For further detailed suggestions for these two scenarios and a number of others, including shopping malls, fire stations, circuses, hair salons, and pet stores, see Jane Davidson's *Emergent Literacy and Dramatic Play in Early Education.*

Props
and Other Multisensory Stimuli

Most early childhood educators are familiar with the concept of object-based learning, whereby a learning experience is initiated by introducing children to a significant object. The process involves multisensory examination, followed by discussion and play. The object serves as a dynamic learning tool, stimulating dialogue and critical thinking. The more sensory experiences associated with the object, the stronger the imprint on the child's memory (Hannaford 1995).

One example of object-based learning is in the abbreviated theme-based drama "A Trip to the Beach" (Chapter 3). Children begin by examining a very large sea shell, brought in by the teacher. They see, smell, touch, and listen to the sounds from within the shell. "Autumn Leaves" (Chapter 7), begins in a similar fashion, with children examining the look, smell, and feel of autumn leaves before launching into a more extended dramatization.

In this chapter, however, we will look beyond using objects to initiate learning experiences to discovering ways in which they contribute to a young child's cognitive and linguistic development throughout the drama experience. After explicating the use of props, this chapter explores other modes of multisensory learning, including the kinesthetic learning potential of sign language. Beyond correlating these techniques with cognitive development, increased concentration, and information retention, the chapter details how each facilitates participation, self-control, and classroom management.

Using Props

From the beginning of time, object transformation has been an essential part of children's imaginative play. A pile of stones becomes a herd of cows; sticks are tied together to make a horse. Today's children still call these symbolic objects "toys," just as they do the store-bought ones de-signed to simulate the real world objects they represent. In the context of classroom drama, however, we refer to these objects as "props."

NONREPRESENTATIONAL PROPS

This section focuses on the value of props that are not lifelike replicas but rather require children to use their imaginations to create verisimilitude. In "A Trip to the Beach," the teacher asks the children to superimpose an image of a tool onto the straws she has just handed out. The specific object transformation might be suggested by the teacher or, better still, come from the child's own imaginative engagement within a specific dra-matic context—in this instance, the bus breakdown.

Object Transformation and Its Value Picture the two-year-old setting up a play picnic in the block area. She picks up a block, calls it a cookie, lifts it to her mouth, but doesn't bite down. Why not? Because she is able to imagine the block is a cookie without forgetting it is also a block.

Research indicates that when children are engaged in pretend play they imaginatively transform objects to fit the context of their play. En-gaged in this kind of activity, they have the ability to hold two represen-tations of an object in their mind at once; that is, they can perceive the block as a block *and* as a cookie at the same time. Yet, when children are not engaged in pretend play, they find it difficult to identify an object in two ways at once. The same two-year-old who successfully manipulated block cookies gets confused when asked to identify a candle that is shaped like an apple. "Is it an apple or a candle?" the teacher asks, and the child is bewildered.[1]

When a three-year-old sorts a tray of colored beads and offers them to his classmates as candy, knowing full well that no one will really eat them, he is engaging in symbolic thinking, a step ahead of the concrete thinking we ascribe to this age.

This "double thinking" is exactly the kind of sophisticated, symbol-making process necessary to read, write, and do math. Written language requires object transformation. Marks on a page have to generate an im-age, the way the block does the image of a cookie. Reading requires that the child project the image of an apple onto a series of marks, (i.e., the word *apple*) on a page. It is a sophisticated process, and dramatic play is one of the ways in which children can practice it.[2]

The Value of Multiple Transformations It is to further this kind of sophis-ticated thinking that we recommend props that invite multiple transfor-mations or interpretations, that is, props that can be interpreted in a number of different ways, such as the flexible plastic straw that can not only be bent into a wrench, but also be fashioned into a screw driver, a flashlight, a jack, or a fuel pump. It is more educationally challenging to give children a straw to fix the bus with when they break down on a imaginary journey to the beach than a box of plastic tools.

Again, this is practice for reading because it is asking children to manipulate the straw in the same way they will soon be asked to manipulate letters to read. In one context, the letter "a" is part of the word *ate*, while in another it makes the word *hat*. The same logic applies to numbers. Reading, writing, and math require a child to take a symbol—a number or a letter—and learn to manipulate it in many different ways.

STRATEGIES FOR WORKING WITH PROPS

It is important to stress that props are not magic wands. A spray bottle alone will not make a successful moment of a weak one. It is your commitment to the spray bottle (as a rainstorm in the Amazon, or a whale's spout) that will make the difference. For this reason, experiment with the specific examples given in this book, but only if they appeal to your creative sensibilities. If you think a bowl of water is an overly predictable way to render a stream (see *The Mud Pony,* Chapter 2), which you feel should be large and full of movement, it's a signal you have something better up your sleeve, something that will work much better for you and your children. The teacher who came up with the notion of using raisins for wasps was so tickled by it that her entire class immediately engaged with her in the image. Your enthusiasm for your own creative connections will be equally contagious, and your students will feel stimulated to make creative connections of their own.

Starting Simple Using props can be as straightforward as using one and two props a session as in *Lance the Giraffe,* Chapter 2, or as elaborate as constructing an entire drama around fine and gross motor props, including masks (see *Sky Woman,* Chapter 5). If you are concerned that your children will find this use of props too challenging, begin by making the object transformations as simple and as accessible as possible. You may even want to be quite directive and start off miming one simple transformation yourself, such as a red scarf butterfly or a straw screwdriver, before handing out a set of props to the class. Maybe it will be two sessions later that you simply hand out a box of straws and say, "Hey! Let's fix this bus."

One problem that sometimes arises is that the children may have no real-life experience of the literal objects you are hoping to represent with the props. In this case, bring in pictures along with your props, or even the real thing. One group had never seen real fish until the teacher brought one in for them to smell and touch. The next day, they used plastic surgical gloves to transform their hands into fish swimming in the ocean.

Another option is to plan dramatic activity in which the prop is easy to identify, such as in the drama of *The Very Busy Spider* (Chapter 7). Yarn translates easily into a spider web. Similarly, when a teacher wears a black glove and runs her hand along the carpet, she instantly conjures up the image of a big, black spider. Yet, even in this simple story drama, the transformations get increasingly complex. In the last session of the Spider drama, glow-in-the-dark stars stand for stars *and* tiny spiders. If this seems too demanding, especially the first time through, you may want to eliminate the double image and let the stars be nothing more than stars. In the next session, you might layer the images—this time the stars transform into tiny spiders cradled in the children's palms.

In our experience, however, nonrepresentational props have worked very successfully, even with children who are apparently functioning at a low educational level. The multisensory appeal of these props immediately absorbs and engages the children, although sometimes it is only half-way into the second session that a child verbalizes the connections—that yarn is a spider web and the gloved hand a spider. Still, never underestimate the power of the imagination.

Once you have had success with the yarn spider web, you might want to use the same prop for something more challenging. One possibility is to weave a dream catcher and use it to talk about dreams in general or weave another web, but this time elicit suggestions from the children as to what it might represent. Some children of course will say, "A spider web!" You could then respond with, "Of course, that's what we used it for last time. But what else could it be?" Broken ice? A bee hive? A many-eyed monster? You might even blow a stream of bubbles across the top of it to represent the dreams themselves. Bubbles that fly away represent bad dreams; bubbles that get through represent good ones (see *The Mud Pony*).

Working with Fine Motor Props Fine motor work—working with small muscle groups, particularly in the hands and fingers—is a vital component of early childhood education, yet there are always those children who shy away from the coloring and craft activities designed to foster these skills. Drama can prove the medium that engages the attention of the most ostensibly uncoordinated child. Many of the tasks, such as manipulating a surgical glove puppet, are open-ended. Each child can make her puppet's movements as elaborate or as straightforward as she wishes. Furthermore, the imaginative dimension of the exercise might propel a child to attempt more ambitious moves than she is usually inclined to.

Let us start with three basic strategies. The first involves handing every child the same prop at the same time—for example, a flexible straw—and letting each interpret it in her own way within a given context, in this case, a broken down school bus (see "A Trip to the Beach").

In the second strategy, the teacher hands out the same prop, but this time she directs the transformations, taking the class through a series based on the changing context of the drama. For example, a paper plate can start out as an airplane seat; in the next scene, it's a fan used to waft away the African heat; in the next, it's something to color while children are listening to a story; and, in the final scene, it is cut in a spiral to become a snake the child can wind around their body and take home (see *Kwa Doma Doma,* Chapter 6). A flashlight can be transposed into moonlight or sunlight, and two beams together make a formidable pair of eyes, especially when they are shone up at the ceiling. Let the children decide, even create, the image.

The third strategy involves the teacher, not the children, manipulating the prop. For example, she might pick up a plastic whirligig noisemaker, and solicit suggestions from the class as to what it might represent. She can then incorporate these into a story sequence where it starts out as the wind, becomes a siren, and finally the helicopter that transports children to a new place (see *The Giant Jam Sandwich,* Chapter 2). (Note: A whirligig noisemaker is usually available at most large toy stores. It is an example of the kind of prop that should only be used by the teacher, because it's unsafe in a child's hands.)

To illustrate and develop these strategies, let us explore an already-mentioned prop—surgical gloves—an item available at most day-care centers (five dollars for a box of sixty at a drugstore or surgical supply store).

At their most literal, they are the kick-off prop for a theme-based hospital drama. Wearing the gloves transforms children into surgeons, nurses, and dentists more economically and efficiently than elaborate outfits. When you introduce the gloves a second time, push for a bigger imaginative stretch. On a day you are working on farm animals, have them blow gloves up into "udders for milking," then turn them into "peacocks with tail-feathers."

If you want to be a little more ambitious, give the children the context but let *them* come up with the images. Travel to the beach and hand out a bunch of gloves, then let children create a shorelife tableau (See "A Trip to the Beach"). They can inflate the gloves into jellyfish, blowfish, or anemones, or leave them flaccid to create squeaky, smelly seaweed. The children can also wear them to create creeping crabs, snapping turtles, and swimming fish. If the children need a jump start, show them some pictures.

Finally, throw a handful of them into the water table and see what wonderful inventions children come up with themselves in the course of water play.

Other examples of fine motor props are

Clothespins and raisins for wasps in *The Giant Jam Sandwich* (Chapter 2)
Feathers for birds in *Stellaluna* (Chapter 2)
Confetti for sunshine in *Persephone* (Chapter 5)

Working with Gross Motor Props Gross motor exercise—working with large muscle groups—is often restricted inside a cramped classroom and is therefore reserved for outdoor play. Again, drama can assist children in practicing gross motor control and coordination because it provides incentive for more inhibited children and structure for the overactive.

When using chairs, tables, and boxes as props, the apparatus involved is usually simply and readily available in most schools. Chairs, tables, and boxes are used in several dramas. Chairs create houses and shops in *Caps for Sale* (Chapter 2). A table makes a cave in "Going on a Bear Hunt" (Chapter 7), and cardboard boxes bring a village to life in "The Stranger" (Chapter 6).

The gross motor prop that is most frequently used in this book is a parachute. Though there is often one available in the P.E. room, most teachers regard it as a high-stimulation piece of equipment that will disturb the settled class and wreak havoc in the active one. The trick is to introduce it gradually, with clear rules and stipulations. For example, any work that involves more than one child in or under the chute must be conducted with shoes off. When one child is taking her turn "swimming" on top, everyone else needs to actively work "the water" for her. It is only fair, it keeps everyone busy, and it burns off any over-the-top energy.

The virtues of the parachute are its versatility and vitality. It can transform from the ocean into the cosmos; billowed into a dome, it can represent the inside of a cave, a circus tent, a chrysalis, a volcano, or a space station. It is the magic school bus without television. Yet even in its simplest rendition, it has the power to intrigue the most reticent children and open up their imaginations.

Logistically, a large prop like the parachute will require some rearrangement of your classroom, such as pushing back chairs or tables. It fits inside a standard room more easily than you think, especially for more low-key drama work.

Further examples of parachute's use are

The ocean in "A Trip to the Beach" and *Sky Woman*
The turtle's back in *Sky Woman*
The belly of a whale in "A Trip to the Beach"
A river and then a tent in *The Mud Pony*
The galaxy in "Space Travel" (Chapter 3)

Setting Limits and Taking Precautions Straws can be used to poke; plastic gloves can be filled with water and dumped on the floor. But then, just about every object in your classroom is open to abuse, especially if proper parameters for appropriate use are not established early on. You need to monitor and regulate the use of a prop exactly the way you would any object in your classroom. "We don't throw chairs at one another, and we don't use the pretend tools to hurt our friends or ourselves."

For this reason, think through ahead of time how a particular prop might be misused in an upcoming session. For instance, if you are going to use a hair dryer for the wind, (see *Persephone*), make sure it has an end that doesn't heat up so much that a child might get burned. If you light any incense or candles, use this as an opportunity to talk about matches, and use deep ceramic bowls as containers. With *The Very Busy Spider* drama, a child might wrap the yarn web around his neck and the rest of the class instantly copy him. Establish this as off-limits behavior before you begin the drama session. Most children are more eager to participate and enjoy the positive benefits of props than to seek attention through abusing them. The child who persists must be asked to sit out the drama (for his own safety), and, in our experience, this is usually sufficient disincentive.

Other examples of props to treat carefully are

Clothespins and plastic knives in *The Giant Jam Sandwich*
Lighted sagebrush in *The Mud Pony* and *Sky Woman*
A fan in *Mirandy and Brother Wind* (Chapter 2)
Any scents or foodstuffs that might cause an allergic reaction

Multisensory Stimulation

Let's go back to the children in Chapter 3 who created the Sand Creatures out of their play in the sandbox. What, if any, is the significance of the sand? Perhaps it is the sensation of sand streaming through fingers that mimics the sensation of fur and claw and weighs down movement, sustaining the image of creatureliness.

Many of the props suggested in this book appeal to more than the visual sense alone. The plastic gloves help stimulate the scene of a hospital through their pungent, reminiscent smell; again their strong smell and slimy texture conjure the image of seaweed; and for *Stellaluna* their texture is reminiscent of both a bat's skin and physical flexibility, while their squeaky sound creates high-frequency bat sounds. Take the parachute and sprinkle glitter into the middle, bounce it, and you've a forest teeming with life or a galaxy of stars.

THE VALUE OF MULTISENSORY STIMULATION

Multiple Learning Styles Additionally, we must respect and address different learning styles. Some children may be stronger kinesthetic learners, and others, more visual, spatial, auditory, or even olfactory. Teachers should aspire to reach every child by creating varying sensory associations that address multiple-learning modes (Gardner 1985).

Associative Networks and Language Assimilation One of the benefits of multisensory props is that they stimulate complex language experiences. Let us take honey, which is used to represent sunshine (see *Kwa Doma Doma*). Squeeze it in a spiral design on a paper plate so that it looks like the sun and is easy to distribute. Honey's golden color is reminiscent of the shiny tint of sunshine, while its stickiness can be associated with feeling hot and sticky on a blistering hot day. Add to this one more dimension—sweetness—the positive feelings we associate with sunshine. Honey is a much stronger way to communicate sunshine than is a picture, because as a whole body experience it compiles not only sight, touch, and taste, but also a range of experiential associations—stickiness, sweetness, and shininess. It fires multiple synapses, underpinning one term, *sunshine,* with multiple language connections and imprints (Hannaford 1995).

Concentration and Recall All this mental activity promotes both immediate language absorption as well as long-term retention. The next time you bring in a plate of "sunshine," ask the children for the words—*sunny, sticky, sweet, delicious.* The time after that, have them recall and mime the sensations without the literal prop in place. After a workshop rendition of the *Sky Woman* myth, a two-year-old went home and retold the complete story to her mother from the collection of props she had compiled during the drama and stored in her paper story sack. The props worked like punctuation marks to propel the child from one segment of the plot to the next.

Despite the delays involved in handing out eighteen strips of colored acetate or spraying eighteen children with water, children will stay focused either through anticipation of the up-coming prop or in its preliminary exploration. When the drama gets going again, they are still very much "in" its atmosphere. Whereas, if they have nothing to feel, taste, or touch, children tend to fiddle with extraneous objects anyway, only these "distractions" tend to move them "out" of the drama orbit.

If a teacher thinks a story through in terms of a sequence of props, he can extend a child's concentration way beyond its usual span.

RECOMMENDATIONS FOR USING MULTISENSORY PROPS

What do you do when the children react to your Amazon shower with shrieks of "Spray me! Spray me! Spray me!"? You ground yourself in the dramatic moment with even more commitment and solemnity than before. "Kayla tree, feel the soothing rain; let your branches dance in the raindrops." If the rumpus continues, you might have to limit the dramatic context. "Remember, trees have roots so they can't walk or run, and trees don't talk" (though, of course, in some imaginary contexts they can do both). Finally, you might want to lower the activity level; for example, you might encourage the trees to "bow" (sit on the floor) and rub the cooling rain into their branches and trunk.

The "Spray me! Spray me!" incident illustrates an important aspect of props in general. They make visible the lapses in focus that are characteristic of this age group. Children move in and out of imaginative worlds with incredible alacrity and facility. Often children who appear distracted by props are actually taking in more information than they would without them.

This raises two important points. First, props are more compelling when children create their meaning for themselves. A boy who has determined by himself that the blue acetate will transport him to the moon is more likely to go there. Second, there are some circumstances in which a specific multisensory prop will prove overstimulating, and despite every effort, the class gets out of control. Try introducing an appealing but lower level prop, such as a taste, with the caveat that they will not get it if they do not sit down calmly (see later discussion of transitions). If that fails, you may have to abandon the drama and try again another day, with a different plan. One bad day doesn't mean you have to give up altogether. Finally, not everyone has to fully believe the spray is an Amazon shower; even literal thinkers can enjoy and remember the experience.

INTEGRATING MULTISENSORY PROPS INTO YOUR ROUTINE

As teachers, we often complain about the daily distractions that work against the efficacy of our teaching; not just noises and visual disturbances, but changes in room temperature—"The children are fussy today because the heating's too high"—and even the smells—"Once they start serving in the lunch room, the children can't think any more. I may as well spare my voice." Children are like barometers when it comes to sensory stimulation, so why not use this sensitivity to your advantage? Multisensory props that are used carefully but appropriately can maximize the educational potential of a dramatic moment, and can even make a dramatic moment out of many routine, commonplace events.

Difficult Transitions Multisensory props can facilitate some of your most stressful classroom transitions. To regroup after a period of dispersed activity, take one of those whirligig tubes (available quite cheaply in dime stores and superstores) and whirl it around over your head. It produces an eerie, foghorn-like sound, pitched just right to stop even the busiest child in his tracks. It is a great way to gather children *without* having to use your voice. To enhance this prop dramatically, give it a pet name. "Oh it's William the wind. You'd better listen; he's blowing up a storm." Or use it as a helicopter blade and summon the children into the helicopter before it takes off for the lunchroom. An umbrella and a spray bottle work well in the same way. "It's raining, guys. Let's gather under the umbrella!"

On a dreary day, squares of colored acetate provide incentives to put on outdoor clothes and go outside. "When you've put on your space suits, I'll give you your red glasses and we'll take a trip outside onto the red planet." Clip a zip-lock bag onto each child's jacket and have them collect "space trash."

The joy and thrill of multisensory props is in the invention of new and different representations. Let the children come up with their own. Hand out rectangles of different colored acetate as the children stand in line at the door, and ask for their suggestions as to where they are going today. Will it be the rain forest, the ocean, or the center of the earth?

One of the hardest transitions can be getting children down to nap. In addition to calming ocean tapes and "nap glasses" (colored acetate), try the multisensory version of the classic *Goodnight Moon* (Chapter 7) as a precursor to nap time.

Props to Facilitate Different Use of Classroom Space Children get used to set places and patterns of classroom use. Occasionally, however, a teacher may want to organize the group differently for a special activity. A flashlight is great for making seat assignments. Shine the light on the floor and tell each child, "This is your spot; please sit on it." It also makes a great alternative to a ruler or pointer when it comes to turn taking: "When I shine the flashlight on you, it's your turn to pick a treat." Alternatively, give each child a paper napkin to demarcate individual space.

They can sit or lie on them. If it is for a drama session, such as "A Trip to the Beach," you can call them beach towels or chaise lounges. This way you can control how close and far apart children are to make sure everyone can participate in the drama without crowding and distracting one another. Later on they could be rafts or surf boards and, finally, pillows to sleep on.

Props to Facilitate Emotional Transitions Pieces of colored acetate work not only to alter the look of a room, but also to transpose the mood. Blue is very calming. If the class is overexcited, have everyone sit in a circle and then hand out blue acetate rectangles to look through and talk about. Red is energizing; green is soothing.

Again, if you have a bunch of frenzied, overextended kids on a day that is perhaps too hot even for outside play, sit everyone in a circle and hand out a bowlful of ice cubes. Let each child physically cool off. They can literally ingest the cool sensation by licking (not swallowing!) the ice cube before rubbing it all over their bodies.

Soothing music is also an effective way of calming an agitated, exhausted, or distressed child, as are therapeutic aromas such as lavender and rosemary.

PROPS TO FACILITATE DRAMA

You have probably already noted that many of the story and theme dramatizations have multisensory props either integrated into the session or appended afterwards. This section explains the method and the rationale behind it.

Getting Started The best way to start using sensory props in drama work is to identify one per session. For example, if a story involves rain or a rainy day, bring in a spray bottle; if it is about winter or cold, use ice cubes. (You can brush each child's forehead with one ice cube if it is not appropriate to hand an ice cube to every child.) If there are flowers in your story, dab each child's nose with perfume. If a story involves food or a meal, work snack time into the story (see *The Giant Jam Sandwich* and *The Mud Pony*).

You can introduce the props either before the beginning of the story or as they occur. The more comfortable you become, the more props you will want to add to your drama work.

Prop Management Props work best when you have organized ahead and have them sitting next to you in an accessible container such as a large basket or a box. Even if you want to make the box or basket available to the children later for dramatic play, you will still want to instruct them to leave it alone during the story circle. For this reason, it is better if the container either has a lid or is large enough so that the children do not see the props in advance.

If you are distributing props to the whole class—for example, strips of acetate—have them counted out ahead of time to make sure you have enough for every child. Once you have finished using the props, you can instruct children to store them either in a pocket or a story sack (paper bag), or you can collect them to hand out again at the end of the day (if they'd like to take them home).

Some props, like confetti, make a fair amount of mess. Build in cleanup time. Have children pick up "sunshine" to glue onto a picture or "jewels" to take home in their pockets. If a prop cannot be recycled, such as cotton balls they have rubbed all over their bodies, build in time to put them into the trash can. In the end, few props will outwit an end-of-day vacuuming or a good wash-up in the sink.

Props to Transform Dramatic Play into a Drama Suppose we had introduced a spray bottle into the Sand Creature drama, and said, "Oh, my goodness, it's raining. What are the creatures going to do?" Maybe the creatures would have drunk the rain or bathed in it, or maybe they would have hurried to look for shelter. Maybe the wetness would have transformed the Sand Creatures into slippery fish. Introducing a new prop injects new imaginative life, not only sustaining a dramatic moment, but helping it to evolve into a story. This story can later be transcribed in story circle, using props to trigger recall. Children can then illustrate the story in groups or individually.

Props to Establish the Setting Multisensory props make wonderful catalysts. They change space. When working with older children, you might pass a globe around the circle and let them trace their travel route with their fingers. If you are moving from a cold place to a warm place, rub ice on the cold and blow-dry the warm.

Let the children close their eyes and rub oil into their foreheads to smell the scents of tropical Africa (see *Zomo the Rabbit*, Chapter 2). It is the smell that transforms the environment and sets the tone for the forthcoming drama.

The simplest sound prop, like a tape of ocean sounds, can evoke the ocean. Add a spray bottle and billow a long piece of blue silk and you have waves and a sea breeze. The forest can easily be established in the same way with a tape of forest sounds, a whiff of pine oil, and a darkened room.

One or two well-chosen multisensory props can transform a child's perception of her environment.

Some of the drama sessions involve extensive multisensory introductions, while others are more straightforward. Adapt these to your own use, keeping in mind that the bigger the cultural and environmental shift required of the drama, the more acclimatization and preparation the children will need to do it justice.

Other examples of multisensory props used to establish setting are

The spray bottle turned to mist for English fog in *The Giant Jam Sandwich*
The flashlight and prism crystal used to create the moon and stars in "Space Travel" and *Persephone*
The stones used to create an island in *Persephone*

Engagement in Role Multisensory props can be used successfully to engage children in role. They enhance the imaginative connection, and whole-body involvement and expand the expressive movement. If children are about to become a flock of birds (see *Sky Woman*), you might give each child a feather and let them tickle themselves into birds. When they tickle their mouths into beaks, remind them that birds do not use the same language as humans—a useful way to contain any over-excited children.

If you are becoming a shoal of fish, you might give each child a taste of saltwater to pucker their faces into fish faces. Give them underwater glasses to look through or long mylar tails to flash. Later, after they have established a sense of role, they might continue without any props at all, or else discover their own.

Other uses of multisensory role enhancement are

Plastic Easter eggs for hooves and face paint for pony markings in *The Mud Pony*
Wax paper for wasp wings in *The Giant Jam Sandwich*
Leaves for deer antlers in *Persephone*
Massage oil for whale skins in "A Trip to the Beach"

Props to Create Full Participation While props can always be used to set the scene, they can sometimes drive a whole dramatic moment, eliciting the participation of an entire class. Let us take this sailing scene (which would fit into *Where The Wild Things Are* or "A Trip to the Beach"). The parachute creates the ocean, occupying any number of children. Use a flashlight to direct six into a boat-shaped configuration in the center of the chute, passing a rope around the outside to delineate the boat itself.

As the ocean gathers momentum, the boat rocks from side to side in the waves. (The children who are not in the boat can manipulate the chute to makes "waves.") A teacher and either an aide or an older child can stretch a long swath of blue silk to make the sail. Any children with physical restrictions can wave a piece of white streamer to make surf or wind, while another can shine a flashlight to make a lighthouse as the storm gathers. A teacher can flicker the lights to create lightning, and Enya's popular song, "Orinico Flow," can produce appropriate crescendos. You might then want to have the boat capsize, while you direct the sailors to swim to shore. Obviously, this sailing scene can fit into many contexts.

Transitions Many of the transitions from lower level to higher level activity, or vice versa, can easily be facilitated with simple props. In *The Mud Pony,* the transition from making the chocolate pudding ponies, a highly stimulating activity, is transitioned through careful washing in "the stream," a bowl of water. This refocuses and calms while being sufficiently appealing in its own right to lure children away from finger painting.

If the activity has been intense, give the children something calming (like a spritz of calming scent, such as lavender) or shine a pool of "starlight" on each one (a flashlight and prism crystal). Have them close their eyes and, either in silence or to the sound of soothing music, prepare them for reentry into their everyday world.

Sometimes you might simply reverse the function of the prop you used to introduce the drama session. The same feather that tickled them into birds can tickle them back to children again. Other examples of props used for transitions are

Glitter to transition from "swimming" to "catching the light" in *Sky Woman*
Ice to simultaneously freeze and calm the winter trees in *Persephone*

Incorporating Sign Language and Kinesthetic Learning

Sign language can be extremely effective with young children (who are often strong visual learners) to reinforce new vocabulary and concepts and to keep children involved and focused. Most drama work is highly visual and physical, and sign language therefore blends in naturally. Following are four basic methods for incorporating sign language into drama work:

1. Use signs in conjunction with speech to clarify new vocabulary.
2. Use signs to create or define a character in the drama session.

3. Transform signs into puppets or objects to be used in the drama.
4. Use signs to illustrate a concept or action within the drama work.

USING SIGNS IN CONJUNCTION WITH SPEECH

Using signs with speech provides children with multiple sensory cues: visual, aural, and kinesthetic. It is not necessary to sign every word being spoken; rather, just sign the key nouns and verbs needed to reinforce main ideas. Incorporate five or six new signs into each session. These can be taught as an introduction to the drama work. Some children respond best to iconic signs (visually representing an object or action). If the standard sign is too abstract, create a gesture that better represents the word. For example, the sign for *dog* is slapping the thigh twice with one hand. However, using two hands on top of one's head to represent the dog's floppy ears creates a clearer image of the dog. Children enjoy creating signs with the teacher. (See Figures 4–1, 4–2, and 4–3 for examples of many of the signs used in drama work described in this book.)

CREATING CHARACTERS WITH SIGNS

Hand shapes are often used in sign language to represent the main features of a person or animal. This idea works well for introducing or describing the main characters in a drama session. An animal's ears, eyes, nose, tail, paws, and body shape can all be defined with gestures, as can its spots, stripes, or feathers. As the children add on each new feature with their hands, they "become" the character, creating a voice to match. This is analogous to putting on pieces of a costume.

TRANSFORMING SIGNS INTO PUPPETS

In addition to becoming a character by adding features, children can use their hands to represent entire characters. The index finger can represent a person, or the hands can be shaped in various ways to represent different animals (turtle, butterfly, birds, bugs, and worms, squirrel, or fish). Children are then free to control the movement or voice of that character.

Typically, more language is drawn from children when they are actually speaking through the hand puppet. Movement and dialogue can be encouraged by such questions as, "Can you make your bird sit in the nest?" or "What do you think the bird said when she saw the broken eggs? Show me." Children often become very involved with a character

a bird in a tree

cat

dog

elephant

turkey

giraffe

turtle

Figure 4–1. Signs for animals

car

train

boat

airplane

helicopter

Figure 4–2. Signs for transportation

that they have created themselves, and ideas for action or dialogue occur spontaneously.

ILLUSTRATING THE CONCEPT OR ACTION WITH SIGNS

By using one hand to sign a tree and the other hand to sign a leaf, the teacher can demonstrate the concept of autumn, as well as the gentle movement of the falling leaf. Prepositions can be clearly illustrated in sign language. Once children understand the concept from the teacher's

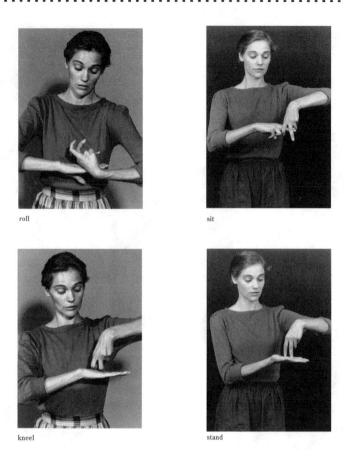

roll   sit

kneel   stand

Figure 4–3. Signs for verbs

demonstration, they can join in the dramatic activity by moving their own hands: "Can you show me the boy standing *in front of* the car?" or "Make the boy tiptoe *around* the tree."

Opposites are also easily demonstrated in sign, and then reinforced with drama and movement. Signs for opposites such as happy and sad, soft and hard, big and small provide a clear visual and kinesthetic illustration. These ideas can then be brought to life by having the children participate in a related drama session.

Signs can be used to create

Hand-puppet animals in *Lance the Giraffe*
Character features in *Bread and Honey, Where the Wild Things Are,*

Caps for Sale, "Preparing for Winter," "Heavy and Light," and *Are You My Mother?*
Environment in *Lance the Giraffe, We're Going on a Bear Hunt, Autumn Leaves, Leaf Journey,* and *Where the Wild Things Are*

Complex as the ideas in this chapter may seem, they are only as sophisticated as child's play. In spontaneous play, children are instinctively drawn to nonrepresentational props, multisensory experience, and the creation of sign and gesture. Five-year-old JJ is sprinkling Parmesan cheese onto his spaghetti. "Look. It's snowing," he exclaims. "Is it really?" his teacher asks. He looks at her with disdain. "In pretend it is." What we have attempted in this chapter is to translate into adult terminology, concepts that are to children as natural as breathing.

Much of the material in this section was conceived in collaboration with Cynthia Matsakis.

Notes

1. In a study conducted by Flavell et al. in 1987, children were shown a candle shaped like an apple. First they were told it was a candle, then they were told it was an apple. When asked, children were unable to name both identities at once. J. R. Searle in his book, *Intentionality*, describes this as "direction of fit." A world-to-mind direction of fit, as exemplified by the apple–candle experiment, seems harder for children to master than the mind-to-world direction that occurs in imaginative pretend play.

2. Contrary to the notion that dramatic play is a diversion from learning, the evidence suggests that when children are engaged in imaginative play they are functioning at the highest cognitive level. L. S. Vygotsky writes in his book *Mind and Society*: "In play a child is always above his average age, above his daily behavior; in it, it is as though he were a head taller than himself" (p. 102).

5

Dramatizing Myth with Young Children

The Power of Myth

This chapter addresses the rich world of multicultural literature and ancient mythology. Previously explored techniques and strategies are applied to this rich body of literature to make it accessible to today's children.

WHAT IS MYTH?

Ancient Tales Myths come from a time in human history when there was little scientific and technological knowledge available to make sense of things. Imagination and observation were the only available resources. Thus these stories evolved, in part, to explain and communicate the mysteries and the workings of the natural world. The very stories that evolved to communicate truth before the scientific revolution read like fiction after it.

Archetypes What most distinguishes myths from stories is their archetypal characters.[1] These characters, such as the inner child, the great mother or father, and the trickster, often have heroic and supernatural capacities. A myth poses a fundamental life-and-death dilemma that effects not only the protagonists' physical existence, but also, usually, their spiritual existence; it then attempts to resolve this dilemma through the interplay of plot, character, and landscape.

In addition to the myths developed here, some of the stories in Chapter 2 also have mythic qualities. *The Giant Jam Sandwich,* for example, is mythic in its exaggerated proportions and in how (albeit in a comic way) it grapples with a life-and-death crisis. *The Mud Pony* involves supernatural forces, and while the little boy in the story seems all too human in his

106

impoverishment and vulnerability, the issues he's dealing with are, sadly, universal.

Myth and Young Minds

ADAPTABILITY

One of the keys to a more child-centered mythology is to appreciate its innate flexibility, to remember that mythology is essentially an oral, not a written, tradition. These were the stories that survived because they were passed down from generation to generation, from storyteller to storyteller. But an oral tradition is also a performance tradition which means that while the shape and theme of each story remains the same through history, each teller tailors the details to his own individual artistry and to the sensibility and needs of the audience at hand.

THE DEVELOPMENTAL FIT

It's not just its "plasticity"—its adaptability—that makes mythology appealing to young children. The content and characters of myth resonate not only imaginatively, but also developmentally. Myths are populated with monsters, dragons, gods, goddesses, heroines, and heroes—the kind of archetypal characters that are omnipresent both in fairy tales and on network TV. If superheroes weren't inherently appealing to this age group, why would the networks rely on them?

Bruno Bettelheim, in his book *The Uses of Enchantment* (1977), discusses the centrality of fantasy and fairy tale in young children's emotional lives. Bettelheim writes,

> The fairy tale . . . takes these existential anxieties and dilemmas very seriously and addresses itself directly to them; the need to be loved, and the thought that one is thought worthless; the love of life and the fear of death. Further, the fairy tale offers solutions in the ways that the child can grasp on his level of understanding. (p. 10)

These exaggerated characters and lurching plots are symbols that serve first to frame, then to resolve fundamental conflicts in children's interior lives. While cartoons have much in common with myths, there are important distinctions to be made. Cartoons rely on stock formulae, and clichéd solutions, whereas myths are more individuated. In myth, a child is coming into contact with a story evolved over centuries and is asked to grapple with fundamental questions of human existence.

Although Chapter 6 focuses more on the emotional and psychological dimensions of myth and legend, the stories outlined in this chapter address important developmental issues, issues that the characters raise and the plots then resolve. For example, in The Seven Nations Creation Myth of *Sky Woman,* Sky Woman's qualities—her curiosity, independence, and risk taking—are identical to those that drive young children to explore the world at their fingertips, with all the consequent mishaps, and, like Sky Woman, the young child is dependent on a nurturing environment to support her in her quest. The promise in this story is, "Grow, take risks, and we will be there to catch you. Stay curious and your world will constantly expand."

THE PRESCIENTIFIC NATURE OF MYTH AND YOUNG MINDS

The mind of the mythmaker and the mind of the young child are very much in sync because both are working from an imaginative, prescientific premise. A five-year-old, engrossed in a TV special on the rain forest, turns to her mother and tells her that now she understands why it rains everyday in the rain forest. It's obvious. The forest gets so sad watching all the bigger animals eating all the smaller ones that she sits down and has a good cry. Then she feels better and the sun comes out. As a story, *Persephone* works in a similar way; it anthropomorphizes nature; that is, it puts a human face on a natural event.

The *Persephone* myth documents the cycle of seasons in terms of a human experience that is both memorable and accessible to young children. *Persephone* involves the separation between mother and child and their subsequent reunification, with the understanding that this cycle of loss and recovery will be ongoing. It's the mirror of a young child's experience in day care or kindergarten. Each day, they must separate from their parents to reunite with them at the end of the school day. As one Head Start teacher said, *"Persephone* is a three-year-old's soap opera. It's the perfect picture of their ongoing anguish."

Not that using myth in the classroom precludes science or is antiscientific; it simply precedes science. Let the story stimulate and open up a child's mind; then follow up or fill in with science. In fact, you should focus your drama sessions to specifically forge connections between story and science.

Making Myths Age Appropriate

Some early childhood educators stay clear of myth: There are too many issues of violence, too many adult themes. With the recent proliferation of multicultural literature, however, there's a whole new generation of myths adapted specifically for young children.

ADAPTATION

You might find a myth that looks perfect for your curriculum and suitable for your class' developmental level, if it weren't for one or two sticking points. This is where you have to devise a way to make the inappropriate age appropriate. For example, at the heart of the classical rendition of *Persephone* is a violent abduction, sometimes described as a rape. The version in this book reframes this problematic area for three-year-old consumption. Hades is personified more as a clown than a villain; his purpose is to entertain not terrify. In this way, he personifies the immature aspect of the child and himself; he's the part of her personality that doesn't know the difference between wanting and taking, the difference between impulse and action. Hades' mistake is not that he wants to play with Persephone, but that he hasn't sufficiently well-developed skills to ask; he grabs instead. As the drama progresses, the children's job is to instruct and enlighten Hades, to tell him how he should have behaved in Demeter's garden, how he should have used his words and exercised self-control. Thus, the story gives children a context in which to instruct the impulsive aspect of themselves.

Beyond impulse control, we've interjected another level into the story. Not only should Hades have asked Persephone, he should have asked her mother as well. In this way, the story reinforces the basic tenets of child safety.

The versions of myths in this book underscore any emotional subtext. In the story, Persephone is described as so happy that she grows taller and taller, maturing from the Springtime girl into the Harvest Queen. Conversely, in the underworld, she's so miserable that she shrinks, becoming smaller and smaller until she's no bigger than a tiny seed. Demeter then reclaims this seed from Hades and plants it in her garden, where it grows, buds, and blooms, bringing Persephone's face back to the earth in the center of the first spring flowers.

TELLING AND RETELLING

Another rule of thumb when working with myth or, for that matter, any story that involves disturbing elements, is to tell the story in its entirety before embarking on any larger scale dramatic activity, and to make sure you reinforce its happy ending. Thus, even if the dramatization involves emotionally charged moments, such as the grieving winter trees calling out for the missing Persephone, you have already provided a context, a container in which to put those feelings. Therefore, the children will be able to leave these feelings behind at the end of the session. In fact, if they feel confident of a positive outcome, they are more likely to throw themselves into the tragic moments that occur on the way. It is a good idea to remind them again during the cool-down period that all will indeed be well. The safer children feel with a story, the more willing they are to commit to it.

APPROPRIATE ROLES AND LEVELS OF INVOLVEMENT

Archetypal Roles The characters in myth are larger than life both in emotion and behavior. Though they display human characteristics, their nature is archetypal—it represents more than the individual. For example, Persephone is Spring, and Sky Woman and Demeter are the Great Mother. These characters are charged with powerful energies, which should be kept one step removed from the children themselves; that is, instead of becoming these characters, children should only encounter them. This can be done simply through storytelling techniques, or the characters can be more fully dramatized either as puppets or masks and even played by the teacher or drama specialist. Provided this boundary is observed, children find these characters easy to relate to.[2]

Real-World Roles When you read the reports of myth dramatizations in this chapter, you'll notice that the roles the children act out in the drama reflect the natural phenomena the myths represent. Hence the characters are the symbols, while the children portray the natural events the symbols represent. For example, in the Persephone myth, children act out spring flowers, bugs, winter trees, rocks, and reindeer—the natural flora and fauna that comprise the seasonal changes the story symbolically describes. In the session dealing with Persephone's abduction, the dramatization consists of a scene in which children become the bugs and critters that consume the harvest. They act out the natural correlative of this violent act.

Forging Connections with Masks and Props

MASK AND PUPPET CONNECTIONS

In our *Persephone* sessions, we have capitalized on the connection between the seasons and the story by creating masks for the characters that highlight the season that character represents. The features on Persephone's Spring face are made of blossoms and petals from spring flowers. Her Summer, more grown-up face is composed of roses and fruits. Demeter has, as one child coined it, "a tree growing up her nose"; she has a tree trunk for a nose, branches for a forehead, and roots and soil define her jaw. Hades comes from underground, so his face is decorated with minerals—gold leaf features against a background of clay tones. For the part of the story where Demeter is in grief, we've made a Winter mask from a palette of whites and grays, using dry leaves, acorns, twigs, and burrs to delineate features.

One of the follow-up art projects for children suggests they go on a nature walk to gather natural materials of the season. Later they will use them to compose a seasonal mask on a paper plate. In the fall, leaf stems make eye lashes and eyebrows, acorns make noses, and maple leaves, blushing cheeks and burnished hair. In the Winter, you can use bark and berries, twigs and husks to build the features of a face.

Another of the follow-up art projects has the children making "Persephone seeds" out of walnut shells with a worry doll inside, allowing them to visually connect Persephone with the seed of life. In *Sky Woman,* children's experience of the story drama mirrors the story's primary theme—the expansive nature of both the universe and the imagination. Thus Sky Woman and Sky Man are introduced as doll-sized puppets. As the story progresses and becomes more fully realized dramatically, the roles are brought to life by teachers in costume, and at the story's closing they are embodied in two larger-than-life festival masks.

Myth Dramatizations

Remember these are reports of the way these extended dramas played out in one classroom. If the number of props seems overwhelming, use what feels comfortable.

SKY WOMAN
From the version by Cynthia Matsakis

This is a good choice for the Thanksgiving season, as it is one of the seminal myths of the Northeast native culture, as well as being a story that emphasizes giving thanks to and for the environment.

Story Synopsis Sky Woman and Sky Man live in the Sky World, but Sky Woman doesn't feel comfortable raising her children there. She persuades Sky Man to help her pull up the Sky Tree. This leaves a large hole in the middle of the Sky, and Sky Woman subsequently tumbles through. She is rescued by the sea birds, who set her down on the back of a turtle. Fish bring mud up from the ocean floor, which Sky Woman fashions into a new home for her babies.

DAY ONE

Materials Honey, streamers, incense of lighted sage, a conch shell, a tape of sea sounds, a spray bottle, a puppet show (discussion follows), a strip of blue silk or a blue sheet, colored streamers, a rain rattle, a rattle, confetti, cotton balls.

Introduction The teacher tells her class how the people of the Seven Nations find stories everywhere. They can taste them in the sunshine (she makes a "sun circle" spiral of honey on a paper plate and lets each child taste their own section), feel them in the wind (she brushes each child with a bunch of streamers), and in the evenings, smell them in the smoke that wafts from their brush fires (she lets each child smell but not touch incense or the smoke from lighted sage brush, an herb that is sacred in many Native traditions). They go down to the water and pick up shells from the water's edge—she picks up a conch shell, holds it to her ear, and sings, "I hear a story, I hear a story unwinding." The children join her in this simple musical phrase, and she passes the shell around the circle for them to hear the "sea–story sound" individually.

Storytelling The story begins with the teacher playing a tape of sea sounds, to pick up and expand the sound the children have just been listening to in the conch shell. She then spritzes them with "sea spray" (a spray bottle). Next she asks the children to cover their eyes and listen to the water. "In the beginning," she says, "the World was wet and the World was dark," and with that she darkens the room. With the help of her aide, she billows a long piece of blue silk over their heads to create first a wave, and then the bending roof that divides the sky world from the water world (a sheet would do as well). To illustrate the rest of the story, the teacher has put together a miniature story theatre in a small picnic basket. She uses dolls for Sky Woman and Sky Man, a plant for the tree, a dried grapevine wreath for the hole in the sky, a flashlight for the light, a small white Christmas tree dove for the bird, a stuffed toy for the turtle, papier mâché fish for the fish, and a box of worry dolls for the babies. (You could substitute with what you have available or would prefer to use. Christmas ornament sales are a good source of puppet show props. Feel free to use glove or finger puppets if you wish. If you have enough worry dolls, you could distribute one to each child, but be careful that they don't drop or lose them before the end of the lesson.)

The first day's story theatre focuses on the basic plot to give children a sense of the whole story. The teacher does, however, pass honey around at the beginning to illustrate the sweet sunshine of the sky world, because the sky world will be the focus of the day's drama session.

Drama: Sky World Dance Children dance to a tape of Native American flute music, waving "pieces of the sky"—different-colored paper streamers. The children have chosen yellow, blue, and pink for their sky colors. Children make shapes such as circles, lines, and triangles with their streamers. The teacher then chases the children with "thunder" (a rattle), and they duck down and cover their heads to avoid the rain (made from streamers or a spray bottle). Each child has a turn listening to the rain fall (use a rain stick, available in many nature-themed stores).

Closing Each child is given a handful of "sunbeams" (confetti) to collect after the rain shower and "a cloud" (cotton balls) to sleep on. The cotton is used to rub off drama, the storytelling, and the children's Native American identity so they can return to their classroom selves.

Follow-up Children use the materials they've collected through the drama to construct an individual picture or group mural about the sky. The teacher takes dictation.

DAY TWO

Materials Puppet show, rope, a flashlight, scented leaves, a hula hoop, a spray bottle.

Introduction The teacher begins by transforming the children into the people of the Seven Nations. She instructs them to make their eyes wide "so they will be sharp enough to see what is in front, beside, and behind." She has them softly beat their chests in unison to create the gentle heart beat of the Seven Nations tribes.

Storytelling The teacher repeats the miniature theater, but this time emphasizes the size of the sky tree and how hard Sky Woman and Sky Man have to labor—to push and pull back and forth—in order to pull it up. She builds this into a comic moment with the puppets panting and sweating. Clapping is a motif used throughout the story to express thanks. Alternatively, you might want to use the Native American "gesture-sign" for thank you.

Drama Children act out pulling up the tree. They sit in a circle and pass a heavy piece of rope around to create the circumference of the tree trunk. Looking up, the children see a flashlight shone on the ceiling to represent the top of the tree. They then smell lemon verbena leaves (the leaves from the magical tree, but any herb or potpourri will do) and rub them on their arms and wrists. The teacher guides them through "pulling the tree up by the roots," moving back and forth with the rope in their hands, pulling then pushing. As the "trunk" sways, so does the "tree top" (flashlight). Finally, the children are encouraged to lean back and "kick up their roots" (feet) as the aide gathers up the "tree trunk." The teacher shows them the hole that the tree left behind (hula hoop). The children clap and thank each other for their efforts.

Closing Children find sleeping places near "the hole" as they listen to the sounds of the dark, wet water beneath (sea tape). A little "sea spray" washes each child back to their classroom and their everyday selves.

DAY THREE

Materials Feather duster or a bag of feathers, puppet show materials, a rattle, a string of bells, Audubon bird call, hula hoop, a flashlight, a tape of music to fly to, a spot light, black construction paper, white chalk.

Introduction The teacher brings in and distributes a bag of colored feathers "to tickle children awake." They tickle their noses to awaken their smell, their ears for sound, mouths for taste, and eyelids for vision. (Use a feather duster if you want to avoid using individual feathers. You can't be as detailed, because you have to move faster around the circle, but it's less messy. If you think holding onto the feathers through the puppet show will be too distracting, collect them in a "nest" [basket] and redistribute.)

Storytelling The teacher has the children recall the beginning portion of the story through question and answer. She then emphasizes the segment of the story where the light pours through the hole in the sky and touches the dark, wet water with life. The teacher darkens the room and shines a flashlight through the wreath. She then directs the light at each child in turn, giving them the name of one of the sea creatures whose eyes are touched with sight. This list includes dolphin, seal, manatee, whale, shark, and tuna.

Children hold onto their feathers throughout the puppet show, so they can now use them to make the sea birds flying up. Sky Woman's falling is accompanied by a rattle, and the birds' flying by a string of bells.

Drama The teacher uses the feathers to tickle the children's bodies into birds. Feet become claws, pants become scrawny bird legs; tails sprout as arms change to wings, and fingers to wing tips. Finally, children transform their human faces, into bird faces replacing their mouths with beaks, after which they have to speak like birds. A bird call is a useful way to help each child find their "bird song."

Children then line up and practice flapping their wings for flight. Any child who breaks into conversation is reminded to keep their bird voice. The room is darkened, and each child "catches a piece of the light" (flashlight beam) in their "wing tips" (palms). Several immediately open their hands and the teacher tells them, "See! You've lost it! Better catch some more." They are then charged to carry "the light" down to the dark, wet water. Each "bird" then takes a turn "flying" through the "hole in the middle of the sky" (hula hoop) as the teacher and the aide gather them around the waist, twirl them around, and send them "flying off" through the room. (If the children are too big and/or too heavy for the teacher to lift without strain, have them jump through the hula hoop to simulate the takeoff into flight.) ("Walking Through the Air," from the soundtrack of Raymond Briggs' *The Snowman*, is evocative flying music.) A single lamp shone against the wall creates shadows both on the walls and the ceiling which enables children to see their flying bird selves reflected around the room. Children in wheelchairs, or with other restrictions that make swinging around or being pulled through a hoop unsafe, can be gently spun in their wheelchairs or have the hoop put over them.

Closing Each bird lands on "a rock" (circles of black construction paper) and folds herself in her wings. Several children still have their "wing tips" tightly clasped. The teacher and the aide go around and ask each bird to open their wing tips and release "the light" onto a rock. They mark each spot with white chalk. Feathers are again used to tickle the birds back into people.

Follow-up The teacher draws an outline of each child's hand on the black construction paper "rocks." This brings together the notion of bird and human, as the hand shape made with fingers closed and thumb opened resembles a bird, the chalk functioning in this context as an eye as well as the light.

Day Four

Materials A hair dryer, feathers, hula hoop, a costume for Sky Woman, Hershey Kisses, a green parachute or blanket for the turtle.

Introduction The teacher turns on a hair dryer and uses it to "warm up the children's muscles" so they'll be ready to catch Sky Woman.

Storytelling The emphasis in this retelling is on the birds catching Sky Woman and looking for the right place to put her down. The teacher throws the Sky Woman doll from child to child, instructing each one to be careful not to drop her. She uses a siren whistle to create Sky Woman's screams. This time, though, she builds a cameo role for the turtle who "clug-clug-clugs" up from the bottom of the ocean and tells the birds to put Sky Woman "right here on my back." They enjoy repeating the turtle's words as well as his avuncular tone, and then mime his gesture, patting their own "turtle shells" (backs).

Drama The teacher repeats the previous day's flying section, miming feathers this time, though, instead of using real ones. The aide keeps the birds occupied while the teacher puts on her Sky Woman costume in the corridor—a large dress, a red clown wig, and rouged cheeks, with Hershey Kisses in her pockets. (A simpler costume would do just as well.) She then turns the lights on and comes running into the room, swinging a whirligig as a visual and sound cue for falling. She cries out, "I'm falling! I'm falling! Come on, you birds, rescue me!" At first, "the birds" stop dead in their tracks until they finally realize that Sky Woman is calling to them. The aide encourages the birds to each take hold of Sky Woman, while the aide herself carries the bulk of Sky Woman under the shoulders. The birds actually carry her over to the "turtle" (a green bunched-up parachute) and lay her down on his back. The children are quiet but obviously flushed and excited and eagerly hug Sky Woman as she thanks them, first signaling the thank you sign, then distributing "kisses" to all. When they've eaten their kisses, they discover they still have "a little piece of the light" (foil wrapper) in their wing tips.

Closing "The birds" curl up in the green folds of "the turtle's shell" (parachute fabric) and rock themselves to sleep, making the turtle sway in the waves, and Sky Woman rubs their backs, singing her favorite lullaby. Gradually, she rubs them back into children and then takes off her own costume, narrating her own transformation from Sky Woman back into their teacher.

Follow-up Children each take a piece of dark-colored construction paper and some bright chalk and draw a picture of the birds catching Sky Woman, accompanied by appropriate music. The teacher then takes dictation.

Day Five

Materials A double zip-lock bag of mud, surgical gloves, treasure (explained later), spray bottle, salt, colored acetate or cellophane, confetti or large glitter, paper plate shells, parachute or large sheet, Sky Woman costume.

Introduction The teacher begins today's class by passing a zip-lock bag packed with mud around the circle for each child to squeeze and describe.

Storytelling The teacher again encourages the children to direct the storytelling up to the point where the fish go down and explore the ocean floor. The teacher distributes a box of surgical gloves, and each child wears the gloves to make a fish. She also brings in a bag of underwater treasures to show children what the fish might find on the bottom of the ocean—a string of pearls, a star fish, colored clam shells, and so on. Finally, the fish take a mouthful of mud, swim up, and scoop it off onto the toy turtle's back.

Drama The teacher transforms the children into fish by having them taste a handful of "sea water"—a sprinkle of salt and a squirt of water in their palms. The grimace becomes their "fish face." She then gives out "underwater glasses" (rectangles of transparent blue acetate or cellophane). After recostuming herself as Sky Woman—in full view of the children this time—she tests the "sea water" herself, with her toes. She sends "the fish" down, so she spreads out "the ocean" (parachute) for them. She directs them to dive underwater and bring back whatever they can find on the ocean floor. Sky Woman and the aide spread out the parachute, turn on a sea tape and let children "swim" under the parachute. After a suitable swimming period has elapsed and some children are showing signs of becoming overstimulated, they lift "the wave" off the fish and calm them by sprinkling "underwater jewels" (a handful of glitter) over each, directing them to cover their eyes with their acetate glasses to avoid getting glitter in their faces. *This was a quiet, compliant class, so no one hurt anyone else or got too overstimulated. However, were this the case, Sky Woman could direct them to go exploring either individually or in pairs.* Each fish is then given "a shell" (a scalloped segment of a paper plate) in which to collect their jewels. The fish then "surface" with both jewels and a handful of mud (mimed).

Closing After their long swim, the fish take their shells to the table and decorate them with brown crayons (mud). They glue on their jewels. The class then washes up, washing themselves back to school children as Sky Woman takes off her costume and becomes their teacher again.

Day Six

Materials Decorated sea shells, Sky Woman and Sky Man costumes, confetti or glitter, cotton balls, lipstick, large masks.

Introduction Children pass their decorated shells around the circle and describe their contents.

Storytelling The teacher gives the children the chance to enact the final puppet show themselves. She divides the scenes and characters up so that everyone has a turn to come up front and manipulate the props. After the story is complete, the teacher opens up the box of worry dolls and counts out Sky Woman's babies on her palm. She then has the Sky Woman doll clap her hands and give thanks to everyone in the story.

Drama The teacher repeats the fish exercise and dresses herself as Sky Woman again. This time, the fish only mime bringing up the mud and jewels. Sky Woman instructs each fish to take hold of the "turtle's shell" (the parachute) and spread it out. Then they mime throwing "mud and jewels" on top as the aide sprinkles some more glitter into the parachute and dims the lights. She tells them the glitter is the electricity that will generate the new earth. As the glitter sparkles, Sky Woman leads the children in the song, "I feel the earth, I feel the earth unwinding" (the same tune as "I hear a story"). As they're singing, they walk in a circle with the parachute. Sky Woman asks them to be quiet and listen, to lay the parachute down and sit on its edge. "You," she says, solemnly seating herself in the center of the new earth, "are the children of the new earth. Let me count you, for you are my new-born babies." Next she counts each one of her children.

Closing Sky Woman calls Sky Man (her aide dressed in a bowler hat and an umbrella to fly with) down from the sky world to meet his children. His gift to them is a cloud pillow to sleep on. Then Sky Man and Sky Woman sing their children to sleep with a lullaby and give each a kiss on the cheek (a dot of lipstick) as they bid them and the story good-bye. They encourage the children to join them in naming the details of the story and saying good-bye. At this point, the two pick up two large full-face masks so that the children can open their eyes and say good-bye to these characters one last time. The teacher and the aide walk around holding the masks so the children can individually touch and speak to the characters. Everyone has something different to say to them, from "I will miss you" to "I hope you take good care of those babies."

Follow-up Let the children develop creation stories of their own. Such as, why the sun goes down at night.

Other Teachers Made These Choices

- Teachers have envisioned the underwater world differently. One had the children "swimming" under a sheet of clear plastic while a bubble machine blew a stream of bubbles over the top. Another used wands of blue and silver mylar to create fluorescent fish and had the children dance with them. Another placed her class around a large bowl of water and had them blow into it with drinking straws.

- Another teacher imagined the final session more explicitly: She had the children get under the parachute, billowed it into a tent shape, and had them "get born" through the hole in the center while a parent pulled them out the other side.

- Instead of using masks, one teacher created a puppet show with doll puppets. She bought a styrofoam sphere and painted one half green and the other brown. One half was the summer–spring world and the other, fall–winter. As she told the first half of the story, she stuck the spring world with ornamental flowers, fruits, and birds. As the world turned cold, she rotated the sphere, pulled out the spring–summer features, and stuck the brown half with ornamental winter trees. (These props are inexpensive and can be found at a craft store.)

- This story has worked well in special needs situations, especially if the children are already used to story dramatization. It is best to abbreviate and/or simplify the story. You might want to leave out the underwater journey or else do the fish very simply. If it is a small group of children with special needs, they can be individually guided through many of the activities.

PERSEPHONE

From the version by Cynthia Matsakis

This story is an excellent vehicle for teaching the seasons; it also builds a powerful bridge between children's imaginations and the natural world, especially for children who live in urban settings. Much of this material has the feel of Greek tragedy. Though children are not familiar with this form, it works well with the story and children respond well. Some of these sessions could be cut back. Five days, however, feels like a minimum with such a complex story.

DAY ONE

Materials Stones, a long strip of blue silk, hair dryers, honey, a flashlight, a prism crystal, a candle, mylar strips, a tape of traditional Greek dancing music.

Introduction The teacher turns on a sea tape and encourages the children to imagine they are becoming stones and sinking into the sea. She touches a stone to each child's forehead while her aide billows a long strip of blue silk over the crouched children to represent a wave washing over the stones. The teacher then directs children to stand and hold hands, telling them that the stones have joined to form an island in Greece. Next, she blows hair dryers in their faces to represent the warm island breezes that transform them from the island into islanders. "In the mornings, the islanders tasted the sweet sunshine (honey) and fished in the blue seas," she tells them. She has them mime casting their nets and pulling in fish, which children imagine and name. Then the room is darkened to create the evening. Children lie on their backs and look at "the constellations" (a flashlight shone through a prism crystal). "In the night sky," she continues, "the people could see heroes and heroines, gods and goddesses, and they told stories about all their adventures."

Storytelling The teacher lights a candle and tells a simple version of the Persephone story without any props or masks.

Drama Each child unwinds a strip of mylar and dances their own "star story." The teacher plays a tape of traditional Greek dancing music.

Closing The teacher brings the lights back up and directs the stars to sink into the sunlight. Children become the dreamers who have dreamt the stories and are now waking up back in their classroom. They "wake" and give themselves a hug and a kiss on the cheek, whispering their own names to themselves to make sure they're back from their dreams.

Follow-up The teacher has the children draw their "star stories" while she and an aide take dictation.

DAY TWO

Materials Rattle, rain stick, floral scented oil, decorated masks, spray bottle, paper plate faces, lipstick.

Introduction: Spring The children close their eyes and listen for the spring rain. The teacher uses a rattle for thunder and a rain stick for rain. She tells them that, after rain, things get quiet and they should listen for animals peeking out from behind the wet bushes. With their eyes still closed, the children "hear" rabbits and foxes, squirrels and dogs. The teacher directs them to open their eyes and smell the "spring smell" (a bottle of floral-scented essential oil). She asks what color flowers the children can smell, encouraging them to come up with their own color and not to imitate their neighbors.

Storytelling The teacher transitions into this segment by introducing the spring mask of Persephone, asking the children to identify the different-colored flowers. She puts the mask on and off her face so that children can experience the mask both as an object and as the face of a dramatic persona. Next, she introduces the children to the Demeter mask and has them identify the natural flora and fauna on that mask, too. She then tells the rest of the story with the masks held, not worn. Holding the masks like puppets, it is possible to act out the conversations between mother and daughter as well as mime their separation and reunion.

Drama The teacher guides the children through a "seed dance" where they find their "seed place" (belly button) and curl up to protect it in "the ground" (the children's bodies). The warmth of "the ground" makes "the seed" grow, and they stretch out their arms to open up one "leaf" (hand) and then another. She punctuates this "sprouting" with dramatic exclamations of "Pow!" They are each given a little scented massage oil to rub onto their "sticky bud" faces and are encouraged to try and stretch "the bud" open. Finally, the teacher gives each a "spring shower" (spray bottle). Again, she makes this more dramatic by making the spray a surprise, so that the children's faces do literally open like flowers. Paper plates scalloped into petal shapes with the centers cut out are passed around to represent flower faces. Each child is now a full bloom swaying in the sun to springtime music (Andreas Vollenweiders' *Behind the Garden—Behind the Wall—Under the Tree* is a good album for gardens). Some children have to be reminded to keep their "roots in the earth." The teacher dabs each with a "fragrance" (scent) and a "bloom" (dabs of lipstick on each cheek).

Closing The young Persephone comes to smell the flowers in her spring garden. The teacher does not wear the mask, but holds it. As Persephone names each flower—lavender, pansies, petunias, and so on—she bids them good night and they curl up in the ground. The teacher darkens the room, and each child makes a pillow of her "flower face" plate. As the children wake, they separate from their flower selves and recall the process involved in growing from a seed to a flower. They then stand up, bidding "their garden" good-bye.

Follow-up Children decorate their flower face masks with crayons, streamers, and glitter.

DAY THREE

Materials Masks, hair dryers, massage oil, baby powder, spray bottle, fruits and vegetables, a large brown blanket or quilt.

Introduction: Summer The teacher blows "warm summer breezes" on the children's skin with hair dryers and protects their skin from the sun's hot rays by using rose-scented massage oil. She has them create "bees" with their sticky thumbs and forefingers, then flutter their other fingers to create "butterflies." The "butterflies" then dip their "tongues" (thumb and forefinger) into "pollen" (baby powder). The "butterflies" kiss themselves on their cheeks and noses, and then kiss each other before flying away. After waving good-bye to their butterflies, each child rubs their "remembering place" (their foreheads or noses, whatever they choose as the place that helps them remember) to recall the image and color of their own individual butterfly.

Storytelling The teacher retells the story, referring to the masks on sticks behind her. She focuses on Persephone's maturing from childhood to girlhood, using gesture and mime to emphasize Persephone's vitality— her running, jumping, and rolling. She stresses how happy Persephone was in her garden, so happy that she grew taller and taller (mimed), until she became the Summer Queen. She introduces the Hades mask, talks about its colors and emblems, and then uses it (hand-held) to mime Hades' abduction of Persephone to the underworld, emphasizing his mistake in grabbing instead of asking. "He liked her so much, and wanted to play with her so much, that instead of using his words and asking if she wanted to play, he simply grabbed her and took her with him."

Drama Children "plant" Persephone's summer garden of fruits and vegetables, using real produce and a large earth-colored comforter. Then they hide the Persephone mask in the "garden" and guide the teacher (as Demeter) in a game of hide-and-seek.

Closing Persephone falls asleep in her garden, and the tired children join her. A "summer shower" (spray bottle) washes them from the imaginary world back to the classroom.

Follow-up As this is summertime, the teacher takes her class on a summer nature walk to collect materials to make summer masks.

DAY FOUR

Materials Sandpaper, garbage-bag twists, pictures of insects, masks, drinking straws, silky cloth, "bug" music (Miles Davis' *Tutu* album works well), fruits and vegetables.

Introduction The teacher bring in squares of sandpaper to make "bug sounds." Each child imagines the different bug that might make these sounds with either their wings or legs. She then gives each child a garbage-bag twist and has them wind and shape it around their finger to make a "bug." She brings in a book of insects to give them ideas. Children then make their own bug sounds and fly their bugs into the air to make "a swarm." After this, they take the twists off of their fingers and pile them in the center of the circle to make "a bug nest."

Storytelling The teacher retells the beginning of the story with the masks, using a question-and-answer technique. She modulates her voice to create character voices, though she still holds the masks on sticks. Later in the story, she emphasizes Hades' abduction of Persephone, focusing again on his failure to use the correct approach when he wanted to play. She then makes sure she emphasizes the reunion of mother and child at the end of the story so the children will be assured that Persephone does eventually return home to her mother.

Drama Children become "big bugs," using drinking straws for bug mouths and face paint on their eyes. They "slither" along their "bug path" (a long piece of silky cloth) to the garden they planted the day before, and "suck up" the nectar and juice from the fruits and vegetables through their straw suckers. They then "slither" back to their "underground bug nest" (circle) with their "full bug tummies" and lie on their backs, kicking their "bug legs" in the air.

Closing The "full bugs" fall asleep in their nest, and the teacher narrates them through the cycle of weaving cocoons and hatching back into children.

Follow-up The teacher does a science activity on the life cycle of bugs.

DAY FIVE

Materials Blue streamers, feathers, masks, pine essence, spotlight, ice.

Introduction: Fall The teacher uses long strips of blue streamers to create the autumn breezes blowing leaves off the trees. First the children use their hands to mime falling leaves, tumbling then skittering along the ground, calling out, "Persephone." Then they each pick a feather and mime a bird practicing flight, then joining the other birds in a flock before flying south, cawing, "Persephone, Persephone," as they go.

Storytelling The teacher holds up the Persephone mask and guides the children in a version of the story from Persephone's point of view. This version of the story also focuses on the period after the abduction, specifically on Demeter's grief over the loss of her daughter. Again, the teacher takes the children all the way to the happy ending of the story.

Drama The teacher puts a little pine essence on their noses so they smell like trees. Their feet become roots, their bodies trunks, their arms branches, and their fingers leaves and twigs. She then darkens the room and uses a spotlight to create a shadow of each "tree" on the walls so they will see the transformation complete. She plays some autumn music (Keith Jarret's *Spirits* album), and the trees sway in the fall breezes while she puts on the Demeter mask and wanders among them, calling out for her daughter. Demeter touches each "tree" with ice (an ice cube) to freeze them into winter trees.

Closing The "frozen trees" gradually melt into children.

DAY SIX

Materials Masks, ice, white scarves, thorns, wild grasses, musk scent, antler-shaped leaves or cutouts, silver tape, a blanket, a blue sheet, a stuffed toy, trail mix or granola, cool water, masks, a music box.

Introduction: Winter The teacher rubs the children's foreheads with ice, and they gradually "freeze all over" before shrinking into "balls of ice," which she covers with "snow" (white scarves).

Storytelling "The ice cubes" melt their faces and hands to listen to the story, which focuses on Demeter's journey over the frozen earth in search of her missing daughter, Persephone. She emphasizes the "thickets of thorns" by bringing in a branch of thorns, the muddy bottom pools with wading gestures, and the swishing grasses with a bouquet of wild grasses. She also stresses the participation of the hungry animals who traveled along with Demeter on her journey.

Drama "The ice balls" roll to the bottom of the hill, stretch out their arms, and call for Persephone. From the hallway, Demeter (teacher in mask) echoes their call. She then enters, and they all listen for their frozen heartbeats. "This is the cold time, the frozen time," she says, "but still Demeter's heart is alive and beating. Her heart moves all of us and we must all move together—the deer, the goats, the antelope. We must go in a herd and travel the earth, searching for Persephone, searching for Spring." Demeter and the aide then turn the children into a herd of hungry winter animals by giving each a little musk scent on their noses and a pair of leaves that are shaped like antlers. They travel around the frozen earth (the classroom organized into a landscape)—along a "precipice" (a line of silver tape down the edge of the carpet), around a "cave" (a table draped with a blanket) with a "hungry beast" inside (a stuffed toy), and across a "stream" (a strip of tin foil). They stop for a snack (trail mix) and break the ice to get some frozen water (cool water in cups). Finally, they hear Persephone's singing voice under the ground (a music box).

Closing Reassured that Persephone is near at hand, "the animals" sleep by the stream. They wash their faces in the cool water to turn themselves back into children.

Follow-up Children attach their leaf antlers to deer masks.

DAY SEVEN

Materials Masks, plastic echo mike, colored rocks, incense, red acetate, a worry doll in a walnut shell, blanket or parachute, perfume, green crepe streamers, confetti, spring music, lipstick, a hand mirror.

Introduction: The Underworld The teacher uses an echo mike to dramatize the echoey sound of the underworld. She brings in colored rocks to demonstrate the different minerals one might find. She lights incense and uses it to represent the smell of the underworld.

Storytelling The teacher focuses on the story from Hades' point of view. She makes him comic and helpless by making him sneeze and then need assistance from the children, who fetch him a tissue. He asks, "What did I do wrong?" They all tell him—by now they remember the story well. He then shows them what has become of Persephone in the underworld; she grew so sad she got smaller and smaller until she turned into a little seed, and he shows them the seed (half a walnut shell with a cotton ball stuffed inside and a worry doll laid on top). The teacher then holds the Demeter mask and modulates her voice to tell Hades that Demeter knows what to do with a seed. She turns to the children to ask them, and most of them know to plant it in the ground. They also know what happens next—that Persephone will grow up with the spring flowers.

Drama Children imagine the ice mountain that makes the doorway to the Underworld. After miming the mountain, they slide their hands to its base and lift it up with great effort. After Demeter has distributed red glasses (strips of red acetate) to see through the Underworld smoke, children follow her down the steps (mimed stepping) to Hades' kingdom. They discover Hades sitting on a hot rock, weeping (aide in the mask), and Demeter asks why he's so sad. He shows them "the seed," and

Demeter asks the children who it is. "Persephone," they reply. "Why has she got so small?" Hades asks, and the children explain, "She wasn't happy in the Underworld. You should have asked her first if she wanted to play, and asked her mother, too." Feeling very sorry about what he's done, Hades gives the seed to Demeter so she can take it back into her garden and make Persephone grow again. Demeter leads the children back into her garden (circle-time rug), where she instructs them to curl up and find their own seed places (as in Day Two). The seeds are covered with a "blanket of winter snow" (blanket or parachute), given "a promise of spring" (dab of perfume), and then encouraged to start "growing." Eventually, they get tall enough to pound and beat on the blanket until it "melts" (is lifted off). The "seedlings" are handed "green shoots" (strips of green streamer) as confetti is thrown over their heads.

Closing As they sit to gather the "sunshine" (confetti), the Persephone mask is carried in so they can experience Persephone walking among them and greeting them by placing a little "bloom" on either cheek (lipstick dab). A mirror is passed around so each "spring flower" might see the face of Persephone in their own center.

Follow-up The children make "Persephone seed dolls" with walnut shells and worry dolls.

Suggestions for Further Development

Once a teacher or drama specialist has decided on a myth, the next step is to identify the themes the story addresses and look for ways to highlight them through storytelling, dramatization, and follow-up. In the bibliography, there is a list of recommended books of myth for further dramatization, including Bible stories such as Noah's Ark and Jonah and the Whale, as well as myths from Central America, Mexico, South America, and the Caribbean, with their less widely known but equally dramatic cosmologies.

Is dramatizing myth worth all the extra work involved in adapting and planning the material? In our experience, myth not only strikes a profound chord with young children, but also sticks. Children remember these stories for years after they have experienced them in the classroom. If you are concerned about time, teach your required curricular units through this drama work—colors, shapes, prepositions, and so forth, can easily be stressed in any number of places. Children's involvement in the story makes them more, not less, receptive to any new information.

The material in this chapter was developed in collaboration with Cynthia Matsakis.

Notes

1. Jung described the collective unconscious as consisting of mythological motifs or primordial images to which he gave the name "archetypes." Archetypes are not inborn ideas, but "typical forms of behavior . . ." (Storr 1983, 16).

2. In Chapter 6, we encourage children to identify with characters like Max and the boy in *The Mud Pony* as surrogates for their own emotional experience. While these stories have mythic qualities, these characters are human children, not supernatural beings.

Drama for Emotional Growth

Much of the material presented in this book is emotionally charged, and moments are emotionally intense. *Stellaluna, The Mud Pony,* and *Persephone* deal with separation as well as emotional and material deprivation. There is both anger and conflict in *Where the Wild Things Are* and near catastrophe in *Sky Woman* and *The Giant Jam Sandwich.* The character of Emma in "The Stranger" faces illness and destitution.

Teachers have so many issues to deal with in the classroom or daycare setting, that the complexity of exploring issues such as conflict and violence through drama or any other medium seems far beyond their capacity. Though most preschool and kindergarten teachers encourage children to identify a full range of emotions, limited work is done on expressing or resolving those considered negative: sadness, fear, and anger. Some feel that the classroom should be a happy place—sometimes the one place children can come to and feel safe. However, there is a growing movement within the public health and education community that schools and educators must take a greater role in helping children process the complex emotional experiences thrust on them by contemporary life, both at home and in their neighborhoods. There is evidence to support the hypothesis that the greater the emotional stress, the harder it is to learn.[1]

This chapter looks at age-appropriate ways to promote emotional growth through drama. It pinpoints three key elements—developing empathy; processing difficult emotions, such as fear, sadness, and anger; and coming up with positive strategies to relieve these feelings.

Empathy: Identifying Emotions and Feelings of Others

Pictures, particularly detailed pictures and photographs, are a good starting place for the development of emotional intelligence in children. There are subtle cues in a face, including the positioning of the mouth and eyebrows, that provide cues as to how others are feeling.

127

One method frequently used with young children to help identify emotions is for the teacher to hold up two-dimensional drawings of faces depicting various emotions. Children are asked to identify the feeling associated with the facial expression. The follow-up work expands this idea to encourage children to take on the voice of the characters depicted.

PICTURE NARRATIVES

This drama session uses pictures and photos from children's books, adding dialogue for self-expression.

Materials Pictures and photographs depicting facial expressions and body language that indicate strong emotions. Good sources for these kinds of pictures are listed in the bibliography.

Introduction The children have some experience identifying related emotions to pictures and photos. In this drama session they will first use pictures and photos to identify feelings, then become the voice of the person in the picture, and finally share their own feelings with the "picture-narrator." As a warm-up, the children create a gesture (or sign) to physicalize the different feelings of each child.

Part One With everyone sitting in a circle, the teacher holds up one of the pictures and explains that she will pretend to be the girl in the picture and talk about her feelings. Starting with the picture of a very angry looking girl, she changes her voice slightly, becoming the character. "I'm so angry! My brother is always playing tricks on me. He told me he would play with me if I found five flies to feed his pet frog. It took me all morning to find the flies and now he won't play! I'm so mad! Does anyone else ever get tricked or teased by a brother or sister?" This is not actually the story from the book, but the teacher wants the children to know they aren't following the story in this drama work. The children respond, sharing their feelings about being teased.

Part Two Now they get to take turns, picking a picture or photograph and becoming the voice of that character. They start off simply, "I'm sad 'cause I'm crying." Often they begin by copying the teacher's ideas, but with encouragement they elaborate, picking pictures they can relate to and projecting their own feelings onto them: "I'm angry 'cause my mommy had to go to the hospital." Don't be surprised if they reveal information about their lives, of which you were previously unaware. This child's mother had been in the hospital for a week (without any visit) and the teacher was unaware of the situation, which had been affecting the child's behavior.

Part Three Beginning with modeling from the teacher, the children are encouraged to respond to the picture-narrator about the situation. To the child whose mother had been in the hospital, "Oh, you must feel pretty lonely. My mommy was in the hospital once, too." Others are encouraged to share similar experiences.

Closing Children use words to make the character in the picture "feel better," even though the expression of that person cannot change.

Discussion The children talk about how feelings change—people are all sad, angry, or frightened at times, but those feelings go away.

Follow-up The children compile a list of the kinds of things that make them feel better, such as hugs, teddy bears, being sung to, and so on.

Other Teachers Made These Choices

- Children drew pictures of the characters they had portrayed, showing what they looked like after they "felt better."
- The class read and dramatized one of the books after this drama session. Children wanted to know what really happened and were delighted to know the problem had been resolved.
- One group of five- and six-year-old children created a story about one of their characters, imagining and acting out different resolutions to the conflict.
- One teacher introduced colors, tastes, and smells that could represent emotions. Colored gel was used effectively to represent layers of emotions; that is, sadness is often underneath many angry feelings (see *Kwa Doma Doma,* in this chapter, for specifics on multisensory stimuli related to emotions).

Note: For children who have difficulty focusing and paying attention, you may be surprised how this drama work can hold their attention. However, you may have to shorten the discussion time. Common issues that may come up include problems with self-esteem and social acceptance. You may also need to hold up a picture in front of some children and begin the monologue for them. Most accept this help and will often be more motivated to begin, or nod, in agreement with what you've voiced.

Processing Emotion Through Story

Kyle had been identified as an at-risk child. He had a hard time staying focused in his kindergarten class and was prone to aggression and moodiness. His home life was unstable, divided between a grandmother and a mother whose new husband felt ambivalent, at best, toward Kyle. When the teacher first told the story of *The Mud Pony* (Chapter 2), about a deprived Pawnee Indian boy who develops inner strength through his relationship with a magical pony, she was surprised by Kyle's attentiveness. He wasn't the kind of child who usually sat through a story, not without fidgeting and disrupting others. This morning he was rapt. For the next four days, Kyle was the child who strove to sit beside the teacher in the story circle and who raised his hand to answer her questions. In the final drama session, the teacher paused to take in the final moment of the story, in which the boy wakes to find his pony friend vanished at last: "Did the boy feel sad?" she asked. "No," Kyle piped up. "Why not?" "Because the pony left his footprints in the boy's heart," he replied.

The Mud Pony struck a profound chord in Kyle. As referenced in Chapter 5, Bruno Bettelheim describes the healing function of the fairy tale in children's emotional and psychological lives. Many of the more emotionally charged stories in this book can function in a similar way, especially if they are presented with care and sensitivity.

STRATEGIES TO FACILITATE EMOTIONAL PROCESS

A child will feel safe making the protagonist of a story a surrogate for her own experiences, and even acting out dramatic scenes with somewhat frightening or aggressive content, if certain conditions are observed.

Boundaries Between Fantasy and Reality Children feel safe broaching difficult emotional material when the boundary between the fantasy world of the story and everyday reality is carefully observed (see Introduction).

Maintaining Role It's important that children never play themselves in a dramatic scene, especially one with negative content, but instead assume a fictional identity—human or otherwise. In this way, they can safely experience and express aggressive or painful feelings. For example, they become the wasps in *The Giant Jam Sandwich* and sting all "the villagers." In so doing, they vent any pent-up rage and frustration through the surrogates of the wasps, but leave it behind when they return to classroom life.

Avoid Putting Children in Victim Roles While in *The Giant Jam Sandwich* it's fine for children to become wasps and act out "stinging," it's not appropriate for them to "be squished" inside the jam sandwich. In the same way, it is too scary to have them play Sky Woman in the scene when she falls helplessly through the sky. In our version, children play the sea birds who fly up and catch Sky Woman in their wings. In this way, they can experience the drama without being at its mercy. If you do opt to act

out the role of Sky Woman with your class, this scene achieves a beautiful reversal of the status quo. For once, the children are in the role of the
rescuer, with the adult in the role of the rescued. There's a joyous,
slightly stunned sense of celebration and empowerment that ensues.
Kwa Doma Doma might read like a blatant transgression of this rule—
the children get swallowed by a monster, after all. The overall trajectory
of this story, however, stresses the triumph over seemingly overpower-
ing emotions and is designed to integrate and process difficult feelings
rather than leave the children hanging.

Stressing the Positive Outcome If a story deals with challenging emotional
situations, such as Persephone's separation from her mother Demeter,
it's important that children always keep the positive ending in mind (see
Persephone, Chapter 5).

Follow-up Individual teachers can decide when it is appropriate to follow
up with discussions that draw out the parallels between the experiences
in the story and the experiences in the children's own lives. It's important to make this a voluntary process, and not to force disclosure. If a
teacher has concerns about the severity of a child's emotional stress, she
may want to carefully select the appropriate moment to confer with the
child. In Kyle's case, the teacher spoke with the school counselor, who
integrated the story into her work with Kyle and his family.

PUTTING THE FOCUS ON FEELING

Many of the story dramas in Chapter 2 have implicit emotional content and
themes. In addition to issues of discipline, Max's journey prepares the way
for a discussion about dreams and nightmares, as well as positive and negative emotions and behaviors. Having Max as the focus of the drama allows
children to explore sensitive feelings through a surrogate. Once they've
explored the story in terms of Max as opposed to "self," children may not
only feel more confident about shifting to more personal expression, but
also be better equipped with the vocabulary to do so. Once they have understood what wildness means to Max, they are more likely to find a voice
for powerful feelings of their own. You may want to reshape the story dramas with emotional content to make that focus more explicit. The following
version of *Where The Wild Things Are* is an example of how this can be done.
  Each of these parts could easily comprise its own drama session. The
story as a whole, however, describes a complete process—the trajectory
from feeling through defiance, imaginative expression, and finally reinte-
gration into the everyday world. If you do break up this organic flow, you
will need to create your own bridges between the imaginative expression

(as snarling wolves or ravenous wild things) and the more conforming behavior appropriate for classroom society. In the following drama session, a cluster of kids were not ready to give up being wolves until half way through the follow-up art project, which was structured to enable them to transfer their "wolfish selves" onto the wolf pictures they were making.

WHERE THE WILD THINGS ARE
From the story by Maurice Sendak

Objective To help children acknowledge, process, and find appropriate expression for wild feelings.

Introduction The teacher uses the introduction to talk about feelings. Some feelings are sweet (she passes honey around the circle) and some are sour (lemon juice). Children make faces for each feeling state and name different feelings. Not all associate sour feelings with more negative emotions, and the teacher acknowledges the validity of that choice.

Part One The teacher stresses how this story is about a little boy who had a big imagination, and whenever he was feeling sour he would imagine he was a wolf. They act out feeling "wolfish." Each child is given a little "wolf scent" on their noses (eucalyptus lip balm). They listen to tapes of wolves in the wild, then howl at "a blue moon" (flashlight shone through a square of blue acetate). "Can wolves and people live in the same place?" the teacher asks. The children think it through and decide that no, they can not. She then explains that when Max was feeling wolfish, his mother made him separate from the other people in his family. She sent him to his room to be by himself.

Part Two The teacher asks how Max feels all by himself in his bedroom, and a number of children respond: "bad," "sad," "lonely." "Remember," the teacher says, "that Max had a big imagination, and whenever he felt bad or lonely he could use his imagination to keep him company and make him feel better." She gives each child a piece of "imagination" to "unwind" (strips of crepe streamer). Children came up with their own images of the jungle, stimulated by the shapes and colors of the paper.

Part Three For the "wild rumpus," they jump individually or in a line along a strip of bubble wrap. The popping sounds make an unusually vivid rumpus. *Some children are a little intimidated by this freedom of expression, but others joyfully engage in "venting" their "wildness." (Some of the more timid children are keen to work with the bubble wrap again during recess in the playground.)*

Next, the teacher emphasizes the part of the story when the Wild Things threaten to eat Max up and Max says no. "Max has had enough of being a Wild Thing," the teacher says, and turns on a tape of a soft

- -

female voice singing, to represent Max's memory of his Mommy's voice. She guides the children through picking up their Wild Thing masks (paper plate faces) and reenacting this dialogue. (The children are Max, and the masks are the Wild Things.) After saying "no" to the Wild Things, each child turns the mask over and uses it as a pillow to dream himself home to the land of good things (the teacher turns up the volume on the singing tape), where the teacher puts on a wig [or scarf] to become Max's mommy, welcoming the children home with a hug and handing out hot cinnamon rolls or sweet-smelling cookies.

Follow-up The class discusses how Max's mother's emotions changed from when she was angry to when she brought him his supper. They also share their own experiences of how it feels when a parent or guardian is angry, and different ways that could make someone feel better when they are angry or sad. This story is an opportunity to clarify and develop vocabulary for different states of feeling.

Other Teachers Made These Choices

- One class discussed dreams and nightmares. Then children created pictures and stories about their own dreams and fantasies.

Creating Positive Solutions

The story of *Kwa Doma Doma* aims not only to help children process difficult emotions, but also to help them come up with creative solutions to find relief, and, where applicable, resolution. This South African myth was selected because it contains two vital elements: First, it personifies anger in dramatic ways (i.e., the central character is an angry monster); second, through the twists and turns of the plot, it seeks a resolution to this difficult emotion. According to the current thinking on therapy for children, the expression of anger should not be terminal, but transitional. Children need to develop ways of coping with and resolving their inner turmoil. In the dramatization of *Kwa Doma Doma,* the villagers have an opportunity to express their rage toward the monster, but they do not escape until they have a dialogue with him. This conversation addresses not only the feelings themselves, but also the situations behind them.[2]

Kwa Doma Doma
From the story version by Sarah Pleydell

An angry monster swallows a village full of people. In journeying through his body, the people experience a range of new emotions and ways to express and calm them. They learn to rely on and take care of one another. Finally, they encounter the monster's heart and the feelings he experiences. In his brain they have a dialogue with the monster about his feelings, finding ways to release them so that they can escape "their prison." At this point, the monster shrinks and the people grow.

A parachute is used in this drama work to represent different places in the monster's body. See Chapter 4 for a recommendation on handling a parachute with children.

Recommendations for Use This material is emotionally powerful and provocative and should be used with care and respect for the children involved. Its purpose is to empower, not destabilize, and this can occur only if the teachers are mindful of the children's affective responses on a moment-to-moment basis. Any plan for drama work can be tailored—either abbreviated and simplified or extended and amplified—to accommodate the needs of a particular class. For example, if darkening the room proves either frightening or overstimulating, then the light could simply be dimmed. The drama work allows many opportunities for physical contact and reassurance. Be liberal with hugs. If, as happened in one of our classes, an aide feels a child needs to be held in her lap throughout the session, she should follow the impulse.

We also recommend that teachers use this material when they are well into the school year and are already familiar with the children in their classrooms. In this way, they will be sensitized to the kinds of issues their students may have. It is probably a good idea to brainstorm ahead of time about what these issues might be, and to think through the practical ways in which they might be addressed. For example, the child who is afraid of going to the bathroom by himself cannot, given the constraints of staffing, always be accompanied by a teacher. He can, however, go with a classmate or let the teacher know where he is going.

It is also important not to discriminate between the different emotional experiences children offer. A child may feel just as much distress over the toy that gets taken away in class as she does around the sibling who hits. Don't stress one over the other. Let the child determine the agenda.

It is imperative that there be access to, and communication with, a school counselor or mental health professional, if issues of violence or abuse surface.

Objective To name and process negative feelings as well as create strategies to resolve them.

DAY ONE: SOUTH AFRICA

Materials Red acetate, honey, oil, tapestry loops, grapes, paper plates, a parachute.

Introduction The teacher creates a multisensory journey to South Africa. Children create an airplane out of chairs, then look at the hot African sun (flashlight through red acetate) and taste it (honey spread on a plate). They can admire its beauty and gifts but must protect their skin from its rays. (Each child rubs some oil into her skin.) Now they are a Zulu tribe, and the teacher passes around pot holder loops to create jewelry. Each child decides what variety he wants to wear—necklace, bracelet, headband, rings, earrings, or even toe-rings. The teacher then drops grapes into their mouths and hands out paper plate fans to decorate as the children listen to the story of *Kwa Doma Doma*.

Storytelling The teacher focuses on the beginning of the story, introducing students to the villagers' peaceful and contented life in South Africa, a life of joy and plenty.

Drama The teacher cuts the plates into spirals, creating "snake friends," which "the people" wrap around their bodies, name, and whisper secrets to. He spreads out "the river" (parachute), on which the snakes dance.

Closing Children wash off their village-selves with river water. (Use a spray bottle so they can feel river spray.)

Follow-up The teacher hangs the snakes from the ceiling of the classroom, encouraging children to engage in private conversations with their individual snake friends.

DAY TWO: ENTERING THE MONSTER

Materials Lemon juice, a parachute, a spray bottle, butcher block paper, crayons.

Introduction Children taste different feelings, but then focus on the bitter taste of fear (lemon juice). They curl up and shake with fear. The teacher asks the children what makes them afraid. Many focus on being left alone in the dark and missing their mommies. Some mention a fear of gunshots, as there had been a recent shooting in a nearby high school bathroom. The teacher acknowledges everyone's contribution equally and takes dictation.

Storytelling The teacher focuses on the part where the villagers are swallowed and concentrates on the darkness of the monster's mouth and throat and how the new feeling of fear the people experienced there made them shake all over. He stresses how the people were able to comfort each other by rubbing each other's backs, singing their mothers' and grandmothers' favorite lullabies to one another, then closing their eyes to picture their comforting faces.

Drama: Rolling Down the Tongue The teacher darkens the room and rolls up a parachute or blanket into a tongue shape. The "villagers" take turns being rolled up in "the monster's tongue" and sprayed with his "saliva" (a spray bottle). After each child is rolled, the teacher asks the question, "How do you feel?" This is an open-ended question to help children identify their feeling-self, not to elicit a prescribed emotion. He then asks how the people in the story felt when they were swallowed. The children come out with phrases such as "scary," "mad," and "funny." He then asks how the people helped themselves overcome their fear, and most children repeat the solutions already articulated in the story. The teacher reaffirms the importance of, first, telling someone you're afraid and what it is you are afraid of and, second, finding positive images to help assuage that fear. He suggests they look for a safe, quiet place inside themselves. Some find it in their hearts, others in their bellies, and a few inside their heads.

Follow-up The teacher rolls out a long sheet of paper and shapes it like a tongue. Each child draws one of the frightened people or lies down to have their own outline traced onto the "tongue." Then children color or paint the people. The teacher asks how the people feel and writes down the people's thoughts in a thought bubble. He suggests things they have said earlier if they can not come up with them now. If a child is talking about herself, he encourages her to put the solution in terms that relate to her; that is, if she is afraid of scary television, she can tell her parents how she feels and/or decide to leave the room when there is a frightening program on television.

DAY THREE: INSIDE THE MONSTER'S STOMACH

Materials Black plastic garbage bags, styrofoam beads, ice cubes, tempera paint, a parachute.

Introduction The teacher introduces a plastic garbage bag as a visual aid, fills it with styrofoam beads, and lets the children squish and squeeze "the people" with their hands; then they discuss how the people must have felt. He asks them what it would feel like to be trapped in a place you can't get out of, and they come up with a range of responses, from "like being in jail" to "I don't like it." He asks what kinds of things make them mad, and they talk a lot about sibling and peer interactions, and one or two talk about interactions with parents.

Storytelling The teacher focuses on the monster's stomach and how the people gave the monster indigestion. "They got squished and squashed, and they got mad and kicked up their heels and yelled, 'Let us out!.' But good as it felt, getting mad did not get the people out of the monster's belly. In fact, it got even more uncomfortable in there. So they had to think of another way, and this time they held hands, climbed on one another's shoulders and up the monster's backbone."

Drama: In the Stomach The teacher darkens the room and uses a parachute to create the monster's stomach. He guides children into small groups and sits them down either underneath or on top of it. He "squishes" them by pressing down or folding the parachute on top of them. Then children are asked to pantomime what it would feel like inside the stomach, demonstrating anger with their whole bodies. (If you don't want to "squish" your children, have them crowd under a table covered with a blanket. Stomp and pound on the table top. End with the how-do-you-feel question? Then ask how the people must have felt.)

Closing The teacher gives the children ice cubes and has them cool down by painting the people's dance of anger inside the monster's stomach. He uses red and blue tempera paints to dip the ice cubes in. The children work well together and are proud of their work.

DAY FOUR: THE MONSTER'S HEART

Materials Strobe light, red acetate, percussion instruments, paper, crayons, crepe paper streamers.

Introduction The children look at the classroom through colored acetate. They discuss how everything looks and how different colors make you feel. They are getting better at expressing feelings in words. When one child brings up feeling sad, the teacher draws the group out to share the things that make them sad. They repeat information about peer and sibling interactions, and some talk about missing their parents while they're at school. (This drama work can be extended to seven days by adding a journey into the monster's lungs before traveling to its heart. The lungs represent fear and confusion.)

Storytelling The teacher focuses on the part of the story where the people move into the heart. He explains how the people begin to feel the monster's feelings as well as their own. They see the monster's happiness, his fear, his anger, and his sadness. The teacher asks what they think makes the monster sad, and one child suggests he misses his mom.

Drama: Create the Heart The teacher darkens the room and brings in a strobe light, which the children view through pieces of red acetate. (A strobe light works beautifully as the monster's pulse, but should never be used around any child suspected of or diagnosed as having seizures. Use a spotlight instead.) Each child dances the monster's feelings in front of the light. The teacher uses fast drum music, which sounds like a heartbeat. Other children play percussion instruments while individuals are dancing.

Closing After all this excitement, children draw pictures of things that make them feel calm. The teacher lets them choose the colors for themselves and takes dictation. The children lie down next to the pictures and swirl streamers to relaxing music.

A parent reports that one child is having bad dreams about the monster, so the teacher sends home with her the plastic dinosaur he uses for the little monster, so she can keep it under her pillow at night. The child is pleased, and the bad dreams stop.

DAY FIVE: DISCOVERING THE MONSTER'S THOUGHTS

Materials Parachute, soft toys, clay.

Introduction The class breaks into small groups and discusses what makes them feel bad—sadness, fear, or anger. The teacher writes down one sentence for each child and acknowledges each child's contribution, but doesn't comment beyond saying he's glad they told him. The range of responses is vast. One child talks about fighting with a sibling; another tells a long story about a sister who was knocked off her bike that morning and was taken to the hospital. This is the first the teacher has heard of this and reports the information to the principal. He closes the session with a group hug. (This type of sharing many times offers insight into a child's behavior. Some situations may call for consultation with the school counselor.)

Storytelling The teacher emphasizes the journey into the brain, where the people read the monster's thoughts: "How he felt so bad because his stomach hurt, his heart was beating fast, and he had a headache. He also felt bad because . . . " And he reads a list of children's difficult feelings. Then he explains how the people soothed the monster's troubled thoughts by talking sweet words to him and by singing the soothing lullaby their mothers sang to them, and that maybe the monster's used to sing as well. One child pipes up with the idea that maybe the monster ate the people because he missed his mommy.

Drama: In the Brain The teacher billows up the parachute to make the brain. (Children sit inside, holding down the sides with their bottoms.) An adult on the outside reads the list of the children's feelings, using an echo mike to give a "monster sound" to his voice. The children sing a lullaby, and "the monster" grows quiet and goes to sleep.

Closing Children make clay monsters to take home and care for.

Follow-up Between sessions, the teacher and aide discuss reasonable "answers" to address the children's feelings and concerns. For example, it is not practical for every child to be accompanied to the bathroom by the teacher, but they could go in groups and take a cuddly toy with them. Some statements simply need acknowledging, such as, "I feel sad when my mommy goes out to work and leaves me with the babysitter"—"That must feel sad, and I'm sure she feels sad, too."

DAY SIX: THE JOURNEY BACK HOME

Materials Parachute, small plastic dinosaur, heart stickers, charms.

Introduction In groups, children discuss what might make the monster feel better. They draw up a list.

Storytelling The teacher completes the story, emphasizing the final dialogue in the monster's brain and integrating some examples he knows will be used later in the drama. He also stresses the escape through the monster's tears and the happy resolution of the story.

Drama: The Escape The previous session is repeated, only this time children talk back to the monster. They eventually sing the monster a lullaby (one of the things that makes them feel better), and the monster cries happy tears. The teachers then help them escape on the monster's tears (pulling them through the central opening of the parachute).[3]

The teacher talks the children through the end of the story, where the tears cause the monster to shrink. A "little monster" (plastic dinosaur) gives each child a kiss goodnight. The monster then lets each child pat him and say good-bye. He gives each child a heart on a string, with a photo of each child on the back of the heart, as a good-bye present and thanks them for helping him find ways to deal with his feelings.

Follow-up The teacher stays open (as after any session) to children who might "get stuck" in the feelings brought to the surface by this drama work. (Offer lots of physical comfort and be available to talk things over with the child.)

Most drama specialists and skilled teachers who have used drama in the classroom are aware of the therapeutic value of this art form (which has been used for years by drama therapists as an effective medium for working with troubled children). Though drama specialists and teachers using drama in the classroom are generally not trained in therapeutic methodology, drama can safely be used as a means of expression and to open up discussion for problem solving, particularly with a school counselor available to handle serious issues that may arise.

It's hard enough for adults to deal with difficult feelings; this doesn't mean we shouldn't try to help children "express their feelings, learn to avoid and defuse violent situations, help each other control peer violence, and use the very same reasoning and problem solving skills developed by the traditional curricula as tools for violence prevention" (Prothrow-Stith and Quaday 1995, 5).

Notes

1. A 1995 report by the National Health and Education Consortium and the National Consortium for African American Children. Inc., sheds light on just how seriously the problems of violence in the home, communities, and schools affect children's capacity for learning—not to mention the social and emotional well being of our children. The statistics are alarming. Recommendations for very young children include a "variety of opportunities to express themselves—their fears, their experiences, their problems—in play, in art activities, and in other parts of a structured program" (Prothrow-Stith and Quaday 1995, 21).

2. From 1994 to 1999, the Kay Fund for Children sponsored "Singing to the Monster: the use of story dramatization as a medium for fostering the expression and resolution of anger and tension in young children." *Kwa Doma Doma* was developed by the authors for this project, which has been used successfully in preschool classrooms in the Washington, D.C. vicinity and incorporated into the Green Leaf program, CPC Health, Bethesda, Maryland. Green Leaf serves minority children coping with barriers in their lives, such as poverty, abuse, learning disabilities, and substance abuse within the home.

3. What is so wonderful about emotions is that they are really grounded in physical sensation (e.g., sliding out the tears of the crying monster). This comes across in the varying responses of the children, which influence the ending. In one lesson, they help the monster feel happy so the people can crawl out of his smiling mouth.

Involving Children with Special Needs

Many of the drama sessions throughout this book include information on how to adapt certain activities to involve children with special needs. Here, we make specific recommendations that can be applied to such situations. These suggestions have evolved from years of experience in diverse preschool and kindergarten settings. They are included not only for use in the classroom, but also as a guide for adapting other drama work to involve children who have special needs.

This chapter focuses primarily on the use of process drama with children who are language delayed or have disabilities that affect cognitive development. There are also suggestions for involving children with physical limitations. These drama sessions include notes describing how varying needs can be addressed. In addition to specific notes in the text, the following are recommended strategies to use when creating your own drama work.

Adapting Drama for Children with Special Needs

Within each classroom, there is often a wide range in children's levels of functioning. Thus the greatest challenge is to meet the individual needs of each child. To facilitate this task, it may be necessary to set individual objectives for each child. For a child who has difficulty becoming involved in group activity, an appropriate objective might be: Will attend to the drama work for three minutes. Related increments might be: Will volunteer a suggestion for creating the physical characteristics of the character, or will participate as an imaginary character for at least five minutes. A child in the same classroom, with limited verbal skills, would have objectives related to verbal participation within the same drama session: Will give an appropriate verbal response when individually questioned about the drama, or will volunteer an appropriate verbal response to a discussion.

A perfectly sufficient goal is that each child enjoy the drama session. 141

This implies, of course, that a child should never be forced to participate. Often children who appear to be completely uninvolved are actually absorbing a lot of information. The teacher can reinforce this peripheral learning by proceeding as if the uninvolved child were actually an integral part of the drama. For instance, if a child remains seated while the others are dramatizing a story, assign that child a related role that doesn't require action. While others are pretending to be birds searching for food, for instance, the stationary child could be a bird staying back to protect the eggs. Use the child's name when describing the role to the class: "Jenny-bird will be protecting the nests while you are looking for seeds and worms." This is also a good way to involve children with physical disabilities (see next section). If the drama involves children in the role of Native Americans hunting for food, children unwilling or unable to participate could be assigned the task of standing guard. Some might even be recruited to bang the drum at any "sign of danger."

Even if a child does not respond verbally to your comments, don't assume there's no awareness of what you're saying. Just as important, other children will perceive that child as a participant. Whenever you notice the slightest involvement, reinforce it with descriptive feedback, such as: "The other birds are so happy you are keeping their eggs warm." Watch closely for even a subtle physical response, and remark, "Look how carefully Jacob is protecting the nest!"

In addition to supporting individual needs, there are other major adaptations to be made in preparing and leading drama sessions for children with special needs. Review the recommendations for adapting drama to meet the developmental needs of preschool children (in the Introduction). These recommendations are critical when working with young children with special needs. Using repetition and imitation within the drama is particularly important for children with language or developmental delays or learning differences.

In addition to these accommodations, the following steps are recommended:

1. Reduce the length of the overall session and each step within sessions.
2. Create a well-defined introduction and closing routine that will be repeated with each session.
3. Clearly define and reduce the number of imaginary characters and settings.
4. Preplan strategies that facilitate control.
5. Use pictures, sign language, and other multisensory enrichment to support new language and concepts.

SHORTENING THE DRAMA

Many children with special needs have greater difficulties with attention than the average three- or four-year-old child. The length of an entire drama session may last only fifteen to thirty minutes, depending on your particular group. Each segment of the drama session should be no longer than three to five minutes, stopping to regain focus as needed. Changing levels (seated, standing, or lying down) and the type of action (discussed in Chapter 1,) will also keep children involved. Depending on the dynamics of your classroom, however, activity outside of the circle will need to be well structured and limited in length.

Before moving on to more complex drama work, some children with special needs require frequent review. This is important for reinforcement as well as reassurance. For example, if you are planning a story dramatization that will be extended over several sessions, you will probably need to review the whole story (or a summary) at the beginning of each session, even though you are working on only a portion of the story at that time.

INTRODUCTION AND CLOSING

Transitions can be difficult for children with special needs. Create a ritual that clearly signals the beginning and the end of "drama time." A song or short activity, such as putting down a special rug, works well as a routine transition from the regular classroom activity to the drama.

In one preschool program for deaf children, the teacher hangs different banners on the wall. Each banner has a different picture representing the activity, such as storytime, drama, and even free-play time. This type of visual symbol for drama time can be very effective, especially for children with limited language skills or difficulties with attention.

A closing routine for each drama session is also necessary. The opening song could be repeated, with different lyrics to signal the end of drama, or perhaps the "drama rug" could be rolled up and put away. Many of the drama sessions in this text end with the characters "sleeping." When the teacher rubs their back, for example, they are verbally guided from the world of the drama back into the classroom. (See Chapter 1 for more information and ideas on introducing and closing a drama.)

DEFINING IMAGINARY CHARACTERS AND SETTINGS

Some children with special needs may have a particularly difficult time with the transition between reality and fantasy. It is important to clarify for these children what is real and what is imagined. Other children may not have highly developed imaginations and will need constant reinforcement with realistic pictures and frequent verbal reminders about pretending or using the imagination. It is also helpful to provide sensory stimuli that reflect the setting of the drama.

Even though these children may have a difficult time putting themselves in an imaginary world, they may still believe a character portrayed by the teacher. However, the line between imagination and reality is so fine that the teacher must make it clear to the children that she will "return." Even with a clear demonstration of the teacher pretending to be the character, some children may not be able to handle the teacher in a role perceived to be "scary." This should be respected. (See Chapter 1 for further discussion of teacher-in-role.)

PREPLANNING STRATEGIES FOR CONTROL

There are several suggestions provided in Chapter 4 for keeping children involved in the drama work. Here are some techniques that work well with children who may need more specific structure:

- Use a circle formation to serve as a "home base," which will be used throughout the drama session. When children become overexcited, they can be brought back to "home base" and continue the drama work on another level. For example, "birds flying about" can be called back to their "nest" for a nap, or "squirrels hunting for food" can be called back to their tree to bury their acorns.

- Create a motivation for returning back to the circle. Try placing masking-tape Xs around the circle, one for each child. When children lose focus during the session, they are told to find their X. This becomes a game for them and a good control device for the teacher. You can also incorporate the X into the drama, as the bird's nest or the squirrel's tree-top perch.

- Choose a sign or develop a signal for the group that they must remember, such as clapping hands three times or flashing the lights. When the children see or hear that signal, they must stop and then look at the teacher for directions. Directions (such as "freeze," "stop," or "sit on your X") can be given vocally or with a sign or gesture. Tell them these signs are a "secret code," and they'll want to be first to respond.[1]

- When taking a journey or traveling from one space to another within the drama, have children hold onto a rope or long ribbon to keep from losing focus. (See "Space Travel" in Chapter 3.)

MULTISENSORY ENRICHMENT

To encourage optimum learning, every effort should be made to provide a multisensory learning experience for children. Young children (particularly those with language delay) respond well to visual and kinesthetic stimuli. When introducing the characters or environment of the drama, use pictures and drawings that are fairly realistic. Some children may need to refer to these pictures throughout the drama session. Pictures also may be used to demonstrate concepts or ideas that children will be acting out, such as leaves falling from trees or an elephant spraying water with its trunk. If appropriate pictures are not available, simple drawings can be sketched before each session.

In addition to pictures and other visual aids, new words and concepts should be reinforced kinesthetically with a physical motion, gesture, sign, or facial expression (see next section). Combined visual and kinesthetic reinforcement of a spoken word provides a multiple imprint on the child's memory.

Additional sensory stimulation can be provided by incorporating sound, touch, smell, and taste. Consider supporting each new language experience with a sensory one (see section on multisensory stimulation in Chapter 4). For example, in the drama session, "Autumn Leaves" (to follow), an assortment of leaves are brought in by the teacher, and the children watch the different patterns made by the falling leaves. Then they examine the leaves' textures, smells, and colors, and listen to the sounds made as they crinkle leaves in their fists. These sense memories make the word and concept of Autumn easier to recall.

If you are planning to use props within the drama, it may be necessary to use ones that are somewhat realistic. Though using a prop as a representation or symbol for something else facilitates thought and language development, children who have difficulty with information processing may not be ready to make these kinds of connections. The props and sensory stimuli can then be placed somewhere in the classroom for further exploration during free-choice time.

INCORPORATING SIGN LANGUAGE

Many of the drama sessions reported in this book incorporate some use of sign language, either to reinforce new vocabulary, create hand puppets, or help define the features of the characters the children are portraying. Sign language and other forms of nonverbal communication, such as gestures and mime, can be used to initiate verbal language. This is particularly appropriate for children with language delay or specific problems related to communication, who may, therefore, be more comfortable with nonverbal communication.[2]

The use of sign language to enhance language acquisition is generally associated with vocabulary development, or semantics. Drama's relationship to language acquisition is often associated with practice in the use of language, or pragmatics. Combined, they address two predominant aspects of language acquisition. The signs represent the spoken word visually and kinesthetically. The dramatization presents the action visually, aurally, and physically. In tandem, drama and sign provide optimum sensory cues, enriching the learner's memory base. Refer to Chapter 4 for pictures of signs and specific modes of integrating signs into drama and pictures of signs (Brown 1990).

Accommodations for Children with Physical Limitations

The use of sign language and gestures within a drama session also provides a wonderful method for involving children who cannot physically participate in the action. While some children become frogs hopping from log to lily pad, other children may carry out the action with a hand-puppet frog in an environment created from signs and gestures. Other hand-puppets that are easier for children to create are squirrel, bird, butterfly, caterpillar, snake, spider, fish, and turtle. A dance can also be done with just the hands or any other body part.

Participation in process drama is a great way to build self-esteem for all children, and there is simply no reason for children with physical limitations or differences to be excluded. These children can be assigned an important role, such as the lighthouse captain who guides the ship to safety through a stormy sea, or a tree with branches that the other children's hand-leaves fall from. Give children in wheelchairs a special role by using the chair as an integral part of the drama. Journeys though space, the jungle, or any imaginary place can be led by a child in a wheelchair. Wheelchairs also make wonderful spaceships and train engines. Assigning a "special" role to a child is such a wonderful way of fostering self-esteem. Consider this for children in your class who may need extra support in this area.

Drama Sessions

The following are reported drama sessions that were either developed or adapted for use with a special needs class. They include notes [in brackets] describing possible further adaptation.

The first two story drama sessions (from children's classics) are primarily storytelling expanded with simple use of multisensory props and limited dramatization. The simplicity of the drama work makes both stories quite accessible for young children with mild to severe disabilities.

GOODNIGHT MOON [3]
From the book by Margaret Wise Brown

This is a favorite bedtime book for many young children, creating a safe sense of ritual about going to sleep. Another objective of the drama work is to facilitate memory and sequencing.

Materials Realistic picture(s) of a night sky with moon, a flashlight, rectangles of blue acetate (sheets available in art stores), rectangles of red acetate, a prism crystal (available in nature stores).

Introduction Children are shown pictures of a night sky with a moon at the same time the sign for *moon* is demonstrated. (Hold your index and thumb finger, curved to make a C-shape, by your eye; then reach this hand-shape straight up toward the sky.) They copy the sign. The teacher closes the drapes and shines the flashlight on the ceiling to represent the moon. She tells them the story is about the moon, and they discuss its appearance, shape, and color. [If children have never experimented with colored acetate, it may be necessary to introduce the colored squares at this time and let the children experiment with them. Some will need assistance.]

Part One While reading the story, the teacher shines the flashlight on the pages of the book as a reading light. As the book is read, vocabulary is reinforced by presenting the sign for each object in the rabbit's bedroom. After all the objects in the bedroom have been named, she shines the flashlight on some objects in the classroom—the blackboard, chairs, playhouse, and so on. Some children are able to verbally identify the objects. In this way, the bedroom in the story becomes part of the classroom, and the classroom part of the story.

Part Two As the bedroom in the story grows dark, children are given the blue rectangles to be used as goodnight glasses. The second part of the book is read through the glasses, and then children use the glasses to look at the objects in the classroom. [Alternatively, if children have the language skills for this, you may shine the flashlight through the blue acetate to darken the room, saying each child's name and letting them name and say goodnight to the furniture.]

Part Three The teacher repeats this process, using pieces of red acetate imposed on top of the blue ones to make the effect even darker. This changes the room's color from blue to purple, and the teacher uses the story to discuss both color and color mixes. [Some children need help holding the acetate. Many need encouragement or assistance repeating the dialogue in the story.]

Closing The teacher collects the acetate and closes the book, ending storytime. As the children pretend to sleep, she shines the flashlight through the prism crystal to create the effect of starlight and "dream light." She first shines "dream light" on each object, and then on each child, naming and bidding each one goodnight. This story works well just before nap time, enacting the final step with the "dream light" after children have left the circle and lain down on their cots.

Depending on the abilities of the children, you may be able to have all or some take on the role of rabbits. This can be done by simply using signs and hand-shapes to create the most obvious features—long ears, round nose, long whiskers, and furry skin and paws. If appropriate, have them hop around the circle before their "bunny bedtime." [One child with physical limitations was given the special role of "keeper of the light," holding the flashlight while the other rabbits hopped in the moonlight.]

THE VERY BUSY SPIDER [3]
From the book by Eric Carle

This story provides a clear and simple illustration about the hard work and dedication of a spider spinning a web. As the children work to create their own giant spider web in the drama, they also experience the importance of cooperation.

Materials Realistic picture(s) of a spider in a web, flashlight, ball of yarn (or more), plastic fly or a black plastic trash bag balled up with tape, "spidery" music, and adhesive stars (glow in the dark, if possible).

Introduction Children are shown spider pictures, leading to lots of excitement and discussion—almost everyone has a spider story to tell. Then all make spider hand-shapes (also the sign for spider). The teacher puts on a black mitten and shakes the children's hands to turn them into spiders. She shines a flashlight on "the spiders" to make them dance. This group of children is able to practice spider crawling around the space to the spidery music. [You may need to save this until the end, letting them just use their hands as spiders at the beginning.]

Part One Now the spider-children are gathered back into the circle to make a giant web (using the yarn to make a large circle, then tossing it back and forth to create a web pattern). The yarn ball is passed around the circle to make a tight web as the teacher tells the children that the spiders are beginning to spin their silken webs. As the first page of the story is read, they repeat the phrase, "She was too busy spinning her web," then roll the yarn ball across the circle. (Use two balls of yarn if you have a large circle.) The teacher calls the name of the child that is to pick up the yarn, adding "spider" to their name: "I'm spinning my web, Sally-spider. Pick it up!" [Some children may try to wrap the yarn around their necks. Before you start, explain that this is dangerous, and anyone who tries will have to sit out, for their own safety.] This procedure is repeated after every page of the story, so that each child has a turn at tossing the yarn ball across to a classmate. Gradually they are able to see a web forming inside the circle. Extra yarn passing is usually needed to make the web full enough. [Children who have difficulty with coordination and focus may need the teacher or assistant to handle the yarn for them.]

Part Two When the teacher gets to the rooster page of the book, a plastic fly is tossed into the web and caught by wrapping it up tightly in yarn. The teacher gives each child a bug (raisin) to nibble on. Then she narrates how sleepy the spiders get after their big lunch, and lifts the web up over their heads. Children roll on their spider backs and kick their spider legs in the air. The teacher repeats the spidery music, and the children crawl around the circle. [This may be omitted if the children's attention span is limited.]

When the teacher shines the flashlight on them, they must crawl back into the circle. This is a fun game, with good control. [One child in this session had difficulty crawling, so he was asked to stay "at home" and guard the spider babies. He made baby spiders with his hands, and the other spiders went out to collect food for the babies.]

Closing Finally, the spider-children curl up and fall asleep in the light of the moon (flashlight). The teacher narrates how the spiders get smaller and smaller until they turn into spider stars. The children are given an adhesive star, stuck into the palms of their hands, and the teacher instructs them to keep their little spider stars safe for the rest of the day.

Follow-up The teacher saves the children's web by hanging it from the ceiling. Children make spiders out of pipe cleaners or paper plates to hang from this web.

"AUTUMN LEAVES" [3]

The aim of this theme drama is to provide the children with a multisensory exploration of the new seasonal change to Autumn.

DAY ONE

Materials Sequential pictures of an Autumn tree with leaves falling; real Autumn leaves to touch, feel, and smell; a plastic container of wet soil; and "leaf" music"—Vivaldi's "Autumn," from *Four Seasons,* works well.

Introduction It is Autumn and children in this preschool classroom have spent several sessions outdoors watching leaves fall, holding leaf-falling races, and tracing and coloring leaves indoors. The teacher passes around leaves and a plastic container of wet soil to help create a sense of Autumn and of being outdoors. They examine the cool, moist texture, crisp smell, and shiny colors, and listen as they crinkle leaves in their fists. The teacher asks them to close their eyes and imagine they are outside in the woods.

Next, she shares pictures of Autumn leaves and demonstrates the sign for *tree*, using the other hand to make hand-leaves dropping from the hand-tree branches. Children imitate. She also has several leaves of varying sizes, and the children watch the different patterns created when they fall. Then she demonstrates how she can simultaneously make her hand float to the ground like a leaf: She drops a leaf and imitates the flowing motion with her hand. All try this. [Some children need to have their hands guided by the teacher.]

Part One As children move their hands slowly through the air, the teacher says, "Your hands look just like leaves falling to the ground! Let's sit on our bottoms and stick our feet up high in the air. Can you make your feet fall slowly to the ground like leaves?" (Demonstrate, if necessary.) The teacher drops various leaves, as the children try to duplicate the movement with their hands, feet, heads, bottoms, and backs. [Children with physical limitations are asked which part of their body can float gently like a leaf. It may only be an eyelid. The other children follow along, each taking a turn to select the next body part.]

Part Two Now the teacher becomes a tree, and the children all come in close to her using their hands as leaves on the teacher's arm-branches. They need reminding that leaves fall slowly to the ground.

Part Three Showing the children the various shapes and sizes of the real leaves again, the teacher asks them to create a leaf shape with their whole bodies. She encourages creativity by guiding them into trying various ways to make different-shaped leaves: "Look, Carlos is using his elbows to make the points of the leaf! Who can show me a different way to make a leaf shape?" Spontaneously, children begin to twirl and float as their body-leaves fall gently to the ground. [Some children have a difficult time generalizing the concept of *leaf* to their entire body, but they will most likely join in the fun of floating around the room.]

Part Four The teacher turns on the tape recorder (playing Vivaldi) and asks the children to imagine that the music is the wind. They are going to be leaves floating in the wind. "You must be very quiet so you can hear the wind-music. When the wind music gets faster, the leaves twirl and fly around, and they slow down when the music is slow. But, when you hear the wind music stop, all leaves must float gently to the ground." [This needs quite a bit of practice and some demonstration from the teacher. One child with cerebral palsy needs to be guided by an assistant. Children in wheelchairs have someone pushing them to the music as they make a leaf shape with their bodies.] The teacher repeats this leaf-floating fun two or three times. When all children finally fall together with the fading music, she pretends to have a giant rake in her hand: "Look, I have a big rake, and I am going to rake all the leaves into one big pile." All have a wonderful time pretending to be raked back to the circle. They are quite noisy and silly, which is alright for a while, until the teacher finally calms them.

Closing Teacher narrates: "Now it's time for all the leaves to become very quiet and take a long winter nap. Leaves, can you find a nice place on the ground to go to sleep? When I see a leaf that isn't wiggling anymore, I will rub that leaf's back until it turns back into a child again." As they are settling, the teacher quietly (almost in a whisper) reads the poem, "Who Has Seen the Wind," by Christina Rossetti.

"AUTUMN LEAVES: LEAF JOURNEY" [3]

DAY TWO

This drama serves as Part Two of the previous drama, but may also be done independently. It is more abstract than Part One and encourages children to use their imaginations. It also focuses on sequencing, as the children transfer the concept of "falling leaves" to their own imaginary journey story. [If children are not able to create their own journey stories, you may still involve them in the storytelling, ending the drama with a "leaf dance."

Materials A box with one beautiful Autumn leaf and "leaf" music from Day One. You may also want to make a simple drawing that duplicates the setting for the leaf's journey story.

Introduction The teacher reviews the previous drama session with the children. They make the sign for *tree* with one hand and use their other hand to make a hand-leaf fall from the finger-branches. Then whole bodies fall as leaves, slowly to the ground.

Part One The teacher narrates: "I brought something very special today. I have it in my magic story box. Can you guess what it is? Listen carefully to hear this gentle sound." She shakes the box (with the leaf inside) and the children guess different things that could make a very light sound. At first there are only a few responses, so the teacher begins to guide them: "Do you think it's a big heavy rock? How about a butterfly? What else could make such a soft sound?" and so on. She dramatically opens the box and shows them the leaf: "This is one of the most beautiful leaves I have ever seen. And, this is a very special leaf. I found this leaf right on the playground this morning, and when I picked it up, it whispered a story in my ear! Would you like to hear the story of this beautiful leaf?"

Part Two The teacher explains to the children that she will need their help. She asks them to use their hands to make different places in the story. They are eager to help. She shows them how to make different signs for the places in the story: trees, houses, water or waves, a boat, wheat fields or grass, hills, a kite, and a church steeple. Sitting in the circle, the first three children use their hands to make trees. The next two or three create hills with their knees, and two children use fingers to make a tall, wavy wheat field. The next two put their feet together to create a lake, using their hands to make water or waves, and one child uses two hands to make a boat sitting on the water. One child makes a hand-kite. Others use their hands and arms to create housetops above their heads, and the last child in the circle stands up, with his hands making a church steeple above his head. [If there are children with limited language, a simply drawn picture of this setting should be shown as each place is created.]

The teacher asks the children to hold their sign-pictures in place while she narrates the story. As she begins, she moves the real leaf around the circle over their hand/trees, hills, lake and so on.

The story begins

> Once there was a leaf who lived in a big tree. (She holds the real leaf up to her hand-tree.) There were lots of other leaves on this tree and other trees all around. But this leaf was a very curious leaf. That was the problem. All the curious leaf could ever see were lots and lots of other leaves. One day the weather started getting cold. Each day it got colder, until the leaf changed colors. It turned orange and red and yellow. Then one day, a big, strong wind blew the curious leaf off of its tree, and the leaf felt very sad. "Oh dear, now I am going to fall to the ground and I will never ever see anything in the world except other leaves." But then the wind blew so hard that it picked the leaf up high in the air and carried it up above the trees and over the beautiful green hills. "Oh look," said the leaf, "what beautiful green hills."

The teacher continues the story, carrying the real leaf over children's knee-hills, hand-trees, and so on. The leaf dances with the kite, then flies over the water and around a boat. It floats down close to the tall wheat, and the wheat waves hello. As it sails over the beautifully colored roofs, she asks the children to describe the color of their rooftops. Finally, the leaf lands on the point of the church steeple. The child playing the church steeple holds the leaf high up to the top of his hand-steeple.

The teacher continues, encouraging children to call out their place as the leaf passes by again.

The church steeple was so tall that the curious leaf could look back over the town and fields and see everything. The leaf felt very happy. Then the wind started to blow again. It blew and blew and the leaf flew back up into the air and back over the rooftops, grass, water, kite, hills, and trees until it landed right back underneath its very own tree. The leaf was very sleepy from its long trip. But so very happy.

Part Three The teacher asks the children to imagine themselves as beautiful leaves. She asks them to describe their colors, encouraging them to think of unusual ideas: "Any purple leaves? Polka dots?" The same Vivaldi music is played again, and they are asked to imagine that they are floating high above the ground like the leaf in the story: "What do you see?" There is no response at first, so the teacher calls out, "Oh, I see red and green cars! I see a dog! What do you see?" They eventually offer several ideas, including seeing a moving train and elephants with spots. As the music fades, the leaf-children fall slowly to the ground.

Closing The children are gathered back into the circle, where the teacher asks them to talk about their leaf journey. It is important that each child has a chance to talk, so they are divided into two groups, with an assistant listening to half of the stories. If this is not possible, perhaps they could divide into pairs and share their travels as a leaf with their partner.

Follow-up Children draw a picture of their imaginary leaf from their own journey. Some are also able to make a picture of their personal leaf journey.

"HEAVY ELEPHANTS AND LIGHT BUTTERFLIES" [3]

This drama session was developed for a class of children learning the opposites, heavy and light. It begins quite simply, but ultimately requires children to work together as two groups and to create a resolution for the animals' problem. [Separating and working in two groups (elephants and butterflies) can be challenging for some children. Hanging pictures of their animal around their necks helps them remember their group and identify their classmates' animal character.]

Materials Box with miniature elephant and butterfly, realistic pictures of each animal, a block, tissue, hand-drawn or machine-duplicated pictures of each animal (one for each child), and yarn to hang the pictures around their necks.

Introduction The teacher gathers the children into a circle and talks about the meaning of *heavy* and *light*. She drops a feather in the middle of the circle and asks, "Can you make your hand fall like the feather?" This is repeated for other body parts and finally whole bodies glide lightly to the ground. Then the teacher drops a block to demonstrate *heavy* and asks, "Now can you make your hand fall like the block?" This is also repeated for other body parts and then whole bodies fall heavily to the ground.

Part One The teacher now shakes the box with a wooden carved elephant inside. It makes a loud thud inside the box. The children, all very curious, try to guess what's inside. [If many children are offering ideas, call on the child or children that rarely offer any.] After a few tries, the teacher gives them hints. "It's a very heavy animal. Can you think of some big, heavy animals?" Even though one child has already said "elephant," the teacher lets them continue to guess.

Finally, she slowly opens the box and shows them the elephant, passing it around in her hand for each child to see or touch. She teaches them the sign for *elephant* and shows them the picture. The little wooden elephant whispers in the teacher's ear. It wants to know if the children would like to pretend to be elephants. The teacher guides them in creating their elephant bodies, using hand shapes to add on the features (their imaginary costume): big floppy ears, little tail, tusks, long trunk, big round belly, and wide legs and arms. Once their costume is "on," they practice heavy elephant stomping.

Now all the elephants stomp heavily around the room, looking for a river from which to drink. When all the elephants have found some water, the teacher suggests they give an elephant friend a shower. After a short period of "splashing in the water," the teacher gathers them back into the circle by calling out, "Hurry up elephants, come back to the circle! I have a new friend for you to meet. Hurry up and take your elephant costumes off. There is something else in my magic story box!" Children pretend to take each part of their elephant costume off, while the wooden elephant whispers a compliment into each child's ear about their elephant expertise.

Part Two This process is repeated with a butterfly in the box, with the children guessing what light animal might be inside. When the butterfly has been discovered, the teacher shows them how to make a butterfly with their hands. They are also shown the picture of a butterfly and use gestures to create specific features, including the wings, antennas, and spots covering the butterfly's wings. Children then become light butterflies, flying around the room. The "butterflies" are asked to look for a flower to sit on, then fold their wings. Then the miniature butterfly asks the children, one by one, the color of their butterfly wings. She then invites all to follow her, flying back into the circle.

Part Three Now the children are divided into two groups—half butterflies and half elephants. The identifying pictures are placed around each child's neck, as the teacher's assistant takes one group to one corner of the room. They are all told that the heavy elephants have a problem and the butterflies will be asked to help. She encourages the elephant-children to consider what the elephants' problem might be. (Suggestions include an itch behind their ear that they can't reach, just hungry, and no friends—because all the other animals are afraid the elephants might step on them.) After the problem has been determined, the butterflies are informed and must agree on a way to help the elephants. Then, with assistance from the teacher and any helpers, the "butterflies" and "elephants" find a partner and act out the solutions they've envisioned. [This problem solving is somewhat advanced, particularly for children with information processing difficulties. Teachers may need to offer suggestions.]

Closing When the interaction is complete, the teacher calls all "elephants" and "butterflies" back to the circle. They remove their "animal costumes" by taking off imaginary trunk, ears, wings, whatever, and becoming children again. The miniature elephant and butterfly thank them for their wonderful work and say good-bye, returning to the magic story box.

Follow-up Some children choose to use clay to recreate the animals. Others take their pictures that they were wearing around their necks and color these in, gluing on cut-out features. The toy elephant and butterfly are left out in a special area of the playroom for children to explore. Some spontaneously recreate the story during dramatic play time.

More Ideas for Drama

Here are some suggestions of books and themes that are worth exploring. The stories have fairly simple plots, lots of repetition, and developmentally appropriate themes for most young children with special needs.

LANCE THE GIRAFFE [3]
By Victoria Brown

This story drama (described in Chapter 2) has been used with several classes of children with special needs. The activity is limited, but children are constantly involved, with a great deal of repetition. If physical activity must be limited, children can participate fully by using the hand-puppet characters and environment. The theme is about self-esteem and being special.

WE'RE GOING ON A BEAR HUNT [3]
By Michael Rosen, illustrated by Helen Oxenbury

This is a fantastic story for drama, exploring prepositions, sequencing, and awareness of one's body in space. It is simple, with a lot of repetition, and children love making the sounds (Swishy Swashy, Squish Squash, etc.) of the various places explored. Set up different areas of the room for this story: grass, river, mud, forest, snow, and cave. If necessary, take only half of your class on the journey at a time to facilitate control. Cover a table with a blanket and put a teddy bear underneath to represent the bear and its cave. When they discover the bear under the blanket, hold the bear like a puppet, following the children back to home base. This drama is lots of fun and well worth doing.

Closing When the story is finished, use a large blanket or parachute to cover the children for their nap. They may want you to read the story out loud, as they are cuddled up. Discuss what makes them feel safe and ask them to bring in their favorite "cuddly toy" the next day.

Follow-up

- Find opportunities for children to actually walk barefoot through tall grass, mud, and perhaps even a "river" made in the sandbox.
- Create a miniature story setting in the sand table with small plastic figures and a bear for children to play "bear hunt."

THE VERY HUNGRY CATERPILLAR [3]
By Eric Carle

This story so clearly illustrates "metamorphosis" and can be done with very little movement, if necessary. Children can use their fingers to represent the caterpillar eating through the various items (their other hand representing the food). Wrap a pipe cleaner around each child's index finger to create antennas, and dot on caterpillar eyes with colored markers (let the children chose which color). As the drama progresses, the children become caterpillars, crawling about the room. You can also use a long thin balloon, filling it up with air a little more each time the caterpillar has his dinner. The children could use their other hand as a cocoon for their finger caterpillar, or become life-size caterpillars, preparing for metamorphosis. To control "butterfly flight," give children an objective, such as finding a beautiful flower to land on (pieces of colored paper or fabric arranged around the "flying area"). Play gentle music for the butterfly movement to help keep children calm. Ask each "butterfly" to describe her wing colors and flower. [Children with physical limitations can create butterflies with their hands. The hand-butterflies can follow along, as the children stay seated.]

Follow-up

- Gather together two or three sleeping bags. Children can become caterpillars and take turns crawling into the bags as their cocoons. Unzip the cocoon to release the beautiful butterflies.
- Make a Magic Story Box, putting in a miniature caterpillar, a

butterfly, and food props for children to create their own mini-drama.

MORE ANIMAL OPPOSITES [3]

"Heavy Elephants and Light Butterflies" familiarizes children with the opposites, *heavy* and *light*, but the same format can be used for similar dramas. Other "animal opposites" include slow turtles and fast squirrels, soft bunnies' fur and hard horses' hooves, and tall giraffes or long snakes and short little mice. Play music that accentuates the opposite animal movement. After exploring opposite animals through movement and sound, create an interaction between the two groups, preferably one that engages the children in problem-solving strategies.

Closing Bringing the animal characters back to the circle for "sleep" works to calm the children down and help them make the transition back to reality.

Follow-up

- Make a Magic Story Box, including the miniature animal pairs used in the drama. Encourage children to match the opposites in their play.

ARE YOU MY MOTHER? [3]

By P. D. Eastman

This simple journey story about a baby bird searching for his mother can be done entirely by using sign or a combination of sign puppets and acting out. All children can make a baby bird hand puppet (with one or both hands for wings) to begin the story. When the bird begins the search, divide the children into four or five groups of animals from the story. (The bird visits many more, but this can be discussed when the story is read.) Give each child a small picture of their animal to help them identify each other. Use a bird puppet to visit each animal group, asking, "Are you my mother?" At the end, one child can stand to be the crane that put the baby bird back in his nest.

Closing Let the children all become baby birds again, and you be the mother, giving each one a gummy worm or perhaps just a gentle rub on the back. Put them in an imaginary nest and read the story out loud.

Follow-up

- Make a large nest by filling a large box with hay, allowing the children-birds, one or two at a time, to experience the textures and smells. You may also provide them with clay and straw to make a small nest. They can create a baby and mother bird with pipe cleaners, small feathers, and whatever other textured materials you may find.

For children with special needs, drama can be a powerful motivator. Its open-ended nature alleviates anxiety about making mistakes and thus encourages children to cross the threshold from nonverbal activity into verbalization. Teachers who frequently use drama often notice not only growth in language acquisition, but also improved self-confidence, social awareness, fine and gross motor development, and creativity. Select stories and subjects to dramatize that are already popular with the children in your class. One reason children learn from drama is because it is fun, and it motivates them to become involved. This is why drama, as well as other arts activities, is one place where children with special needs can succeed.

Notes

1. Signs also can be used in this way to manage difficult transitions, such as "clean-up time" and lining up, or as a private way of reminding children to share, be careful, or even to flush the toilet.

2. Since the early 1970s, there has been a growing body of research demonstrating significant improvement in language acquisition and language use for certain groups of children when sign language is incorporated into the curriculum. Furthermore, sign language used in this way proves to be more effective than standard language arts programs and some other specialized language treatments. The children can learn new words faster and more thoroughly, and are able to generalize better when instruction incorporates sign language (deViveiros and McLaughlin 1982, Konstantareas 1984, Musselwhite 1986, Brown 1990, Wagner 1998).

Assessment

Assessment can be a valuable tool in improving the practice of drama with preschool and kindergarten children. It can, of course, generate rigorous data to document the value of drama, even in already over-crowded curricula. But, most important, it can create the conditions for continuous teacher-guided program improvements and profes-sional development in the classroom, and give teachers new to drama a sense of direction. There have been several studies, conducted mostly by researchers within the field and by outside assessment groups, that demonstrate the efficacy of drama-in-education, including programs in preschool and kindergarten. In this chapter, we examine age-appropriate methods of assessment that can be utilized by pre-school and kindergarten teachers using drama in the classroom.[1]

Assessment for Instructional Purposes

The National Association for the Education of Young Children (NAEYC) states that in early childhood programs, the primary pur-pose of assessment is to assist teachers in planning instruction for in-dividual students and groups. According to NAEYC, teachers should be the primary evaluators, since they will be the ones to make maxi-mum use of the assessment results. Formal standardized testing is considered inappropriate for this young age group unless it is on an individual basis (NAEYC 1990).

STANDARDIZED TESTS

Educational program assessment ranges from standardized tests to observations and the collection of performance samples. However, when measuring the development of children as young as three, "stan-dardized tests" are considered to be artificial, particularly if the data are gathered in only one time frame or context. Though reliability can be improved by using a large sample, this is not practical for the classroom teacher. At the opposite end of the continuum, "observations over time" can produce more authentic data. Furthermore, data collected by an outside researcher may actually be less reliable than data collected by the classroom teacher, who is more familiar with the individual nuances of the children (Smith 1991).

APPROPRIATE ALTERNATIVES

In many early childhood programs, more "authentic" methods of assessments are being implemented by teachers. These include:

- collections or portfolios of the children's work, including stories they write and paintings
- tape recordings of their verbal recollection of the event
- problem-solving tasks
- general group assessment
- the recording of developmental milestones over time through use of systematic teacher observations and anecdotal records

In NAEYC's general guidelines for assessment of young children, assessment involves a large number of observations of the child in a variety of circumstances. These assessments should be based on real, not contrived activities. The assessment should fit with the goals of a developmentally appropriate curriculum for young children and allow the teacher to obtain information about a child's performance in more than one time frame and more than one context (NAEYC 1990, Patton 1987, and Smith 1991).

Methods for Assessing Drama

INDIVIDUAL ASSESSMENT

In keeping with NAEYC's guidelines for assessment in early childhood education, it is useful to collect a variety of information on children's individual involvement in a drama program.

Portfolios Consider maintaining a portfolio of individual children's progress in drama. This could include any follow-up artwork they do pertaining to a particular drama session, written observations by the teacher, and perhaps some type of recall task.

One recall task that works well with children as young as three, is to have children draw a series of pictures that depict events in the drama session and then dictate captions for those pictures to the teacher. A child's words are written under the pictures, which are stapled together in the order the child has presented them. The child's title for the "book" is written on the front, adding the child's name after "written and illustrated by." This has a dual purpose: stimulating children's interest in writing at an early age and providing a record of their recall of an activity, in this case, drama. The creation by each child of three or four of these books throughout the school year provides some indication of growth.

Although one would expect the books to become more detailed as the children mature, the changes in the drama recall books could be compared with books the children have written for other activities, such as field trips. One simple method for assessing growth with this type of document is to count the number of items recalled for each event. The number of details the child imagines or creates beyond that which actually occurs should also be noted. Process drama often stimulates the child's imagination of events beyond those which actually took place, particularly at this early age. An increasing number of imagined events or details indicates an increase in creativity.

Use of a Tape Recorder Another recall task that can be used for drama assessment, requiring less time than the preparation of a book, is accomplished with the use of a tape recorder. After the drama session, the teacher or classroom assistant takes a child to the side and asks such questions as: "Can you tell me what happened in our drama? What happened first? Then what happened? How did the character feel? How did he solve the problem in the story?" This conversation is recorded and the number of details or events recalled can be tabulated at a later time. Collecting this type of data three or four times throughout the school year provides useful information about the students' memory, concentration, language, and sequencing skills.

This type of "retell task" can be useful in measuring creativity as well as comprehension. In one study comparing children who listened to a story read with children acting out the same story, children who participated in the dramatization of the story recalled more than twice as many events compared with those who had simply listened to the story. This group also added events that did not take place but that they imagined had occurred. (Children in both groups were four years of age.)

Problem-solving Tasks Much of the drama work documented in this text incorporates problem-solving tasks. Keeping a record of children's suggestions for solutions provides useful information about their use of language as well as their understanding of cause and effect. This is not always easy to record because of the spontaneous nature of the drama.

However, a classroom assistant could keep a record of individual responses.

Children's answers to follow-up questions are also useful in this way. "What did you like best about the drama work? What did you enjoy doing in the drama? Was there an animal or person you wanted to be, or would like to pretend to be next time we do this drama? How did Max feel when he returned home to find his supper waiting?" Their responses to these questions, as well as their ideas for problem solving, should be kept in a portfolio along with pictures and teacher's notes about each particular drama session.

Periodic Data Collection The NAEYC assessment guidelines stress that teachers should make ongoing observations of young children. This approach also works well in assessing a drama program. As many written notes as possible should be kept, recording notable changes or growth in the child's drama work. For children ages three to six, observations should focus on aspects of child development that are associated with dramatic play (see the Introduction). Drama will have similar effects on social learning, language acquisition, creativity, emotional and moral development, self-concept, and self-esteem. Cognitive development would reflect specific concepts and themes explored in the drama work.

GROUP ASSESSMENT

It may not be feasible to record details of each child's participation, but, in addition to accounts of individual children who made notable changes or growth, taking time to record thoughts and observations after each drama session can provide pertinent information about the group work. This gives the teacher an indication of an appropriate length of time for the sessions, appropriateness of topics, overall group interest and involvement, and the direction in which the drama work should proceed.

Types of questions for group assessment include the following: Did the children enjoy drama more this session than previously? Are they more willing to participate in drama than they did initially? Are children spontaneously requesting drama time at other times during the school day? Are (more) children more willing to participate within the drama session when asked? Has the amount or rate of spontaneous involvement increased? Has the amount of spontaneous verbalization and dialogue increased? When children have a choice over which book to read, do they more frequently select books that have been dramatized in class over those that have not? Do children extend a story or theme explored in drama during their free-play time? Do they appear to be more creative in their dramatic play during their free play time?

A scale is particularly useful for this type of observation, saving time and making it easy to note change. For example:

> How did student participation in this drama session compare with the previous drama session?
> Only when solicited—Some—Most—Full participation

A more mathematical method for tabulating responses is to provide numbers to circle, from one to ten (considering ten as one hundred percent) below each question. Comparing the numbers at the end of each quarter or half-year helps determine growth (see Table 8–1). A questionnaire can be developed that addresses issues that apply to the teacher's particular objectives, and copies of it can be filled out after each, or every other, drama session. This information serves as a record, with any growth or decline easily detected.

In addition to keeping notes of the students' involvement and growth in the drama, it would be useful for the teacher to make an occasional videotape of their work. This provides a concrete record, not only of the children's involvement, but also of the teacher's growth in administering the drama program.

SELF-ASSESSMENT

If you are interested in measuring your own progress in leading the drama, a similar questionnaire can be developed rating your responses from one to ten, as in Table 8–1. This type of questionnaire can also be used by a drama specialist working in the classroom. Preparing a questionnaire that is tailored to address specific concerns and objectives provides a time-saving assessment tool. This type of form (utilizing a numerical rating) makes it simple to calculate change over time, and also to make comparisons between classes.[2]

Conclusion

For educators and drama practitioners who are convinced that process drama is a powerful tool, assessment is crictial to demonstrate its value and efficacy. Even for practitioners who believe primarily in "art for art's sake," assessment, regardless of the findings, provides useful information about our work. When good data and information are shared, consolidated, and disseminated, the field itself is strengthened and empowered.[3]

Table 8–1   Drama Program: Teacher Questionnaire

1. How frequently did you use the drama with your class?
   a) once a week   _____
   b) 2 times a week   _____
   c) 3 times a week   _____
   d) 4 times a week   _____
   e) 5 times a week   _____
   f) more than 5 times a week   _____

2. On average, how many minutes did you spend on each drama session?

In answering the following questions, circle the number that most closely corresponds to your response to the question.

1. How comfortable were you with using drama in your class?

Not at all comfortable 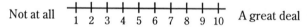 Very comfortable

2. How much did the children enjoy the drama experiences?

Not at all 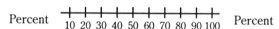 A great deal

3. What percentage of the children participated?

Percent 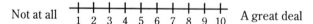 Percent

4. Did your use of the drama program take away time from other important activities?

Not at all 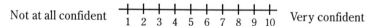 A great deal

5. How confident were you in using drama?

Not at all confident 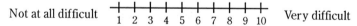 Very confident

6. How difficult was it for you to implement the drama program?

Not at all difficult 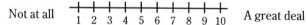 Very difficult

7. How much do you think the children's social skills improved as a result of the program?

Not at all 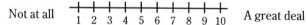 A great deal

8. How much do you think the children's language skills improved as a result of the program?

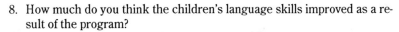

Not at all   1 2 3 4 5 6 7 8 9 10   A great deal

9. How much do you think the children's use of their imaginations has improved as a result of the program?

Not at all   1 2 3 4 5 6 7 8 9 10   A great deal

10. How well were the objectives for the drama work met?

Not at all   1 2 3 4 5 6 7 8 9 10   A great deal

11. How motivated were you to create your own drama material as a result of your experience with the program?

Not at all   1 2 3 4 5 6 7 8 9 10   A great deal

12. How frequently do you plan to use the drama during your next year of teaching?
    a) once a week   _____
    b) 2 times a week   _____
    c) 3 times a week   _____
    d) 4 times a week   _____
    e) 5 times a week   _____
    f) more than 5 times a week   _____

13. In general, how difficult was it for you to implement this program?

Not at all difficult   1 2 3 4 5 6 7 8 9 10   Very difficult

14. In general, how well do you think you implemented the program?

Not at all well   1 2 3 4 5 6 7 8 9 10   Very well

(Brown and O'Donnell 1991)

Notes

1. In 1997 the National Assessment of Educational Progress (NAEP) completed the first national arts assessment in twenty years, and the first ever to go beyond music and the visual arts to include theatre. The youngest students field-tested were in the fourth grade. However, this testing material (available in CD-ROM format) is quite extensive, providing the serious researcher with useful information on the development, administration, and scoring of assessment tasks for the four arts disciplines. "The Field Test Process Report," published in the spring of 1999, could be used to inform the development of field-specific assessment tasks and tools for early childhood. For further information see: *Arts Education Assessment Framework for the 1997 National Assessment of Educational Progress.* Single copies are available free from the National Assessment Governing Board, 800 North Capitol Street, NW, Suite 825, Washington, D.C. 20002-4233. Copies also may be obtained at http://www.nagb.org/pub.html. Copies of *NAEP and Theatre: Framework, Field Test, and Assessment,* NCES 98-528 may also be accessed over the World Wide Web at http://nces.ed.gov/NAEP/.

2. For specific information regarding this method of measurement see *The Measurement of Meaning* by Osgood et al. (1957).

3. This topic is discussed more fully in "Assessment of Preschool Drama Programs," by Brown (1992). For more details on general assessment in early childhood education see: National Association for the Education of Young Children (1990), Bredekamp (1992), Smith (1991), and Patton 1987.

Bibliography

Children's Books

Here are the children's books and other activities referenced (in the order they appeared) in the text, with recommended follow-up bibliography.

Chapter 2: Stories

Cooke, T. 1994. *So Much*. Cambridge, MA: Candlewick Press.

- Brown, M.W. 1972. *The Runaway Bunny*. New York: Harper & Row.
- Ernst, L.C. 1992. *Zinnia and Dot*. New York: Viking Press.
- Hest, A. 1997. *You're the Boss Baby Duck!* Cambridge, MA: Candlewick Press. (And other *Baby Duck* books from this series.)

Cannon, J. 1993. *Stellaluna*. San Diego, CA: Harcourt Brace & Company.

- Asch, F. 1988. *Oats and Wild Apples*. New York: Holiday House.
- Cannon, A. 1996. *The Bat in the Boot*. New York: Orchard Books.
- Eastman, P.D. 1960. *Are You My Mother?* New York: Random House.
- Guarino, D. 1989. *Is Your Mama a Llama?* New York: Scholastic.

Steig, W. 1986. *Brave Irene*. New York: Farrar, Straus & Giroux.

- Brett, J. 1981. *Fritz and the Beautiful Horses*. Boston: Houghton Mifflin.
- Seuss, T.G. 1940. *Horton Hatches the Egg*. New York: Random House.
- Stewart, S. 1997. *The Gardener*. New York: Farrar, Straus & Giroux.

- Williams, V.B. 1982. *A Chair for My Mother.* New York: Greenwillow Books.

Brown, V.L. 1984. *Lance the Giraffe.* Unpublished.

- Cannon, J. 1997. *Verdi.* San Diego,: Harcourt Brace & Company.
- McCully, E. 1992. *Mirette on the High Wire.* New York: G. P. Putnam.
- Small, D. 1985. *Imogene's Antlers.* New York: Crown Publishers.
- Yashima, T. 1955. *Crow Boy.* New York: Viking Press.

Asch, F. 1992. *Bread and Honey.* Milwaukee: Gareth Stevens.

- Flack, M. 1960. *Ask Mr. Bear.* New York: MacMillan.
- Joosse, B. 1991. *Mama, Do You Love Me?* San Francisco: Chronicle Books.
- Pinkwater, D. 1992. *The Big Orange Splot.* Norwalk, CT: Hastings House.

Sendak, M. 1963. *Where the Wild Things Are.* New York: Harper & Row.

- DePaola, T. 1987. *Maggie and the Monster.* New York: Holiday House.
- Mayer, M. 1968. *There's a Monster in My Closet.* New York: Dial Books for Young Readers.
- Sendak, M. 1981. *In the Night Kitchen.* New York: Harper & Row.

Caron, C.L. 1988. *The Mud Pony: A Traditional Skidi Pawnee Tale.* New York: Scholastic Books.

- DePaola, T. 1983. *The Legend of the Bluebonnet.* New York: Putnam.
- Goble, P. 1978. *The Girl Who Loved Wild Horses.* Scarsdale, NY: Bradbury Press.
- Keane, C., and C. Reasoner. 1998. *Prince of the Stable.* Troll Communications, L.L.C., USA.

SUGGESTED STORY DRAMAS

McKissack, P.C. 1988. *Mirandy and Brother Wind.* New York: Alfred A. Knopf.

Slobodkina, E. 1949. *Caps for Sale.* New York: Harper & Row.

Stevens, J. 1995. *Tops and Bottoms.* San Diego: Harcourt Brace & Company.

McDermott, G. 1992. *Zomo the Rabbit: A Trickster Tale from West Africa.* San Diego: Harcourt Brace Jovanovich.

Vernon, J. 1972. *The Giant Jam Sandwich.* Boston: Houghton Mifflin.

Chapter 3: Beyond Story

"Preparing for Winter"

- Carle, E. 1994. *The Very Hungry Caterpillar.* New York: Philomel Books.
- McCloskey, R. 1948. *Blueberries for Sal.* New York: Viking Press.
- Rosen M. 1989. *We're Going on a Bear Hunt.* New York: Margaret K. McElderry Books.

"The PT Birds and the Sand Creatures"

- Pfister, M. 1994. *Dazzle the Dinosaur.* New York-London: North-South Books.

"Space Travel"

- Asch, F. 1993. *Moondance.* New York: Scholastic.
- Gauch, P. 1971. *Christina Katerina and the Box.* New York: Coward, McCann & Geoghegan.
- Holl, A. 1969. *Moon Mouse.* New York: Random House.

"The Hospital"

- Cole, J. 1989. *The Magic School Bus—Inside the Human Body.* New York: Scholastic.
- Houtzig, D. 1985. *A Visit to Sesame Street Hospital.* New York: Random House.
- Rey, Margaret, and H. E. Rey. 1966. *Curious George Goes to the Hospital.* Boston: Houghton Mifflin.

"The Stranger"

- Bunting, E. 1991. *Fly Away Home.* New York: Clarion Books.
- Di Salvo-Ryan, D. 1991. *Uncle Willie and the Soup Kitchen.* New York: Morrow Junior Books.
- Gackenbach, D. 1992. *Claude the Dog.* Boston: Houghton Mifflin.

- Kroll, V. 1995. *Shelter Folks*. Grand Rapids, Michigan: William B. Eerdsman.
- Wolf, B. 1995. *Homeless*. New York: Orchard Books.

"Your Own Backyard"

- Erdrich, L. 1996. *Grandmother's Pigeon*. New York: Hyperion Books.
- Wildsmith, B. 1980. *Professor Noah's Spaceship*. New York-Oxford: Oxford University Press.

"Superhero Alert"

- Rathmann, O. 1995. *Officer Buckle and Gloria*. New York: Putnam.

"The Restaurant"

- Vernon, J. 1972. *The Giant Jam Sandwich*. Boston: Houghton Mifflin.

"A Trip to the Beach"

- Frasier, D. 1998. *Out of the Ocean*. San Diego: Harcourt Brace.
- Norbet Wu. 1993. *Fish Faces*. New York: Henry Holt.
- Sheldon, F. 1997. *Whale Song*. New York: Penguin U.S.A.
- Waters, J. 1991. *Watching Whales*. New York: Dutton.

Chapter 5: Dramatizing Myths with Young Children

Matsakis, C. *Persephone*. Unpublished.
———. *Sky Woman*. Unpublished.

- Janisch, H., and L. Zwerger. 1997. *Noah's Ark*. New York: North-South Books.
- Krauss Melmed, L. 1992. *The Rainbabies*. New York: Lothrop, Lee & Shepard.
- McCaughreau, G. 1992. *Greek Myths Retold*. New York: Margaret K. McElderry Books.
- Pilling, A. 1997. *Creation: Read Aloud Stories from Many Lands*. Cambridge, MA: Candlewick Press.

- Walker, R. 1998. *The Barefoot Book of Trickster Tales.* New York: Barefoot Books.
- Zeldis, Y. 1997. *God Sent a Rainbow.* Philadelphia: Jewish Publication Society.
- Zelinsky, P. 1997. *Rapunzel.* New York: Dutton.

For Latin American myths see the "Fifth World Tales" series by Children's Book Press, San Francisco.

Chapter 6: Drama for Emotional Growth

Talking Pictures

- Grindley, S., and C. Thompson. 1990. *I Don't Want To!* Boston: Little, Brown.
- Polacco, P. 1994. *My Rotten Redheaded Older Brother.* New York: Simon & Schuster Books for Young Readers.
- Reynolds, P. 1991. *King of the Playground.* New York: Simon & Schuster.

Pleydell, S. *Kwa Doma Doma.* Unpublished.

- Gerstein, M. 1986. *The Seal Mother.* New York: Dial Books for Young Readers.
- Seeger, P. 1986. *Abiyoyo: Based on a South African Lullaby and Folk Story.* New York: Macmillan.
- Steig, W. 1969. *Sylvester and the Magic Pebble.* New York: Windmill Books.

Chapter 7: Involving Children with Special Needs

Brown, M.W. 1947. *Goodnight Moon.* New York: Harper.

- Asch, F. 1982. *Happy Birthday, Moon.* Englewood Cliffs, NJ: Prentice-Hall.
- ———. 1983. *Mooncake.* Englewood Cliffs, NJ: Prentice-Hall.

Carle, E. 1995. *The Very Busy Spider.* New York: Philomel Books.

- Aylesworth, J. 1992. *Old Black Fly.* New York: Holt.
- Carle, E. 1977. *The Grouchy Ladybug.* New York: Thomas Y. Crowell.

"Autumn Leaves" and "Leaf Journey"

■   Polacco, P. 1991. *Appelemando's Dreams*. New York: Putnam.

"Heavy Elephants and Light Butterflies"

■   Carle, E. 1989. *Animals, Animals*. New York: Philomel Books.
■   Seuss, T.G. 1954. *Horton Hears a Who*. New York: Random House.

ABBREVIATED DRAMAS

Rosen, M. 1989. *We're Going on a Bear Hunt*. New York: Margaret K. McElderry Books.
Carle, E. 1994. *The Very Hungry Caterpillar*. New York: Philomel Books.
Eastman, P.D. 1960. *Are You My Mother?* New York: Random House.

References

Adamson, D. 1981. Dramatization of Children's Literature and Visual Perceptual Kinesthetic Intervention for Disadvantaged Beginning Readers. Ph.D. diss., Northwestern State University of Louisiana, Natchitoches.

Bergen, D., ed. 1988. *Play as a Medium for Learning and Development: A Handbook of Theory and Practice.* Portsmouth, NH: Heinemann.

Bettelehim, B. 1977. *The Uses Of Enchantment.* New York: Vintage Books.

Bolton, G. 1979. *Toward a Theory of Drama in Education.* Portsmouth, NH: Heinemann.

Bredekamp, S., ed. 1997. *Developmentally Appropriate Practice in Early Childhood Programs Serving Children from Birth Through Age Eight.* Washington, D.C.: NAEYC.

———, ed. 1992. *Researching Potentials: Appropriate Curriculum and Assessment for Young Children, Volume 1.* Washington, D.C.: NAEYC.

Brown, V.L. 1992. "Assessment of Preschool Drama Programs." *The Drama Theatre Teacher* 4 (3): 5–9.

———. 1990a. Integrating Drama and Sign Language: A Multisensory Approach to Language Acquisition and Its Effects on Disadvantaged Preschool Children. Ph.D. diss., New York University.

———. 1990b. "Drama as an Integral Part of the Early Childhood Curriculum." *Design for Arts in Education* 91 (6): 26–33.

———. 1987. (Results of a drama/story retell task on Head Start children, ages three to four). Unpublished raw data.

Brown V.L., and O'Donnell, A. 1991. Teacher Attitude Survey. Wolf Trap Institute for Early Learning Through the Arts. Vienna, VA. Unpublished.

Carlsson-Paige, N., and D.E. Levin. 1990. *Who's Calling the Shots? How to Respond Effectively to Children's Fascination with War Play and War Toys.* Philadelphia: New Society Publishers.

Cazden, C., ed. 1981. *Language in Early Childhood Education.* Washington, D.C.: NAEYC.

Christie, J.F., and E.P. Johnsen. 1983. "The Role of Play in Social-Intellectual Development." *Review of Educational Research* 531: 93–115.

Courtney, R. 1980. *The Dramatic Curriculum.* New York: Drama Book Specialists.

———. 1974. *Play, Drama, and Thought: The Intellectual Background to Drama in Education.* New York: Drama Book Specialists.

Damasio, A.R. 1994. *Descartes' Error: Emotion, Reason, and the Human Brain.* New York: Putnam.

Davidson, J. 1996. *Emergent Literacy and Dramatic Play in Early Education.* Albany, NY: Delmar Publishers.

Dennison, P.E., and G.E. Dennison. 1989. *Brain Gym, Teacher's Edition.* Ventura, CA: Edu-Kinesthetics, Inc.

deViveiros, C.E., and T.F. McLaughlin. 1982. "Effects of Manual Sign Use on the Expressive Language of Four Hearing Kindergarten Children." *Sign Language Studies* 82 (35): 169–177.

Fein, G., and M. Rivkin, eds. 1986. *The Young Child at Play: Reviews of Research, Vol. 4.* Washington, D.C.: NAEYC.

Flavell, J.H., E.R. Flavell, and F.L. Green. 1987. "Young Children's Knowledge About the Appearance-Reality Distinction." *Developmental Psychology* 23: 816–822.

Ford, S. 1993. "The Facilitator's Role in Children's Play." *Young Children* 486: 66–69.

Fromberg, D.P. 1990. "Play Issues in Early Childhood Education." In Seefeldt, C., ed. *Continuing Issues in Early Childhood Education.* 223–244. Columbus, OH: Merril.

Gardner, H. 1990. "Arts Education and Human Development." Occasional Paper 3. Los Angeles: Getty Center for Education in the Arts.

———. 1985. *Frames of Mind: The Theory of Multiple Intelligences.* New York: Basic Books.

Garvey, C. 1990. *Play.* Cambridge, MA: Harvard University Press.

Gazzaniga, M.S., ed. 1995. *The Cognitive Neurosciences.* Cambridge, MA: MIT Press.

Getzels, J.W., and P.W. Jackson. 1962. *Creativity and Intelligence.* New York: John Wiley & Sons.

Goals 2000 Arts Education Partnership. 1998. "Young Children and the Arts: Making Creative Connections." A report from the task force on children's learning and the arts: Birth to age eight. Washington, D.C.: U. S. Department of Education.

Goodman, J.R. 1991. A Naturalistic Investigation of the Relationship Between Literacy Development and Dramatic Play in Five-Year-Old Children. Ph.D. diss., Peabody College, Vanderbilt University, Nashville, TN.

Haight, W., and P. Miller. 1993. *Pretending at Home: Early Development in a Sociocultural Context.* Albany: State University of New York Press.

Haley, G. 1978. Training Advantaged and Disadvantaged Black Kindergartners in Socio-Drama: Effects on Creativity and Free Recall Variables of Oral Language. Ph.D. diss., University of Georgia, Athens.

Hannaford, C. 1995. *Smart Moves: Why Learning Is Not All in Your Head.* Arlington, VA: Great Ocean Publishers.

Head Start Program Performance Standards and Other Regulations. 1998. U.S. Department of Health and Human Services: Washington, D.C.

Henddrick, J. 1992. *The Whole Child.* New York: Macmillan.

Hensel, N. 1973. Development, Implementation, and Evaluation of a Creative Dramatics Program for Kindergarten Children. Ph.D. diss., University of Georgia, Athens.

Jones, E., and G. Reynolds. 1992. *The Play's the Thing: Teachers' Roles in Children's Play.* New York: Teachers College Press.

Kolb, D. 1984. *Experiential Learning: Experience as the Source of Learning and Development.* Englewood Cliffs, NJ: Prentice-Hall.

Konstantareas, M.M. 1984. "Sign Language as a Communication Prosthesis with Language-Impaired Children." *Journal of Autism and Developmental Disorders* 14 (1): 9–25.

Kostelnik, M., A. Soderman, and A. Whiren. 1993. *Developmentally Appropriate Programs in Early Childhood Education.* New York: Macmillan.

Levin, D. 1994. *Teaching Children in Violent Times.* Cambridge, MA: Educators for Social Responsibility.

Linfield, R.S. 1996. "Can Scientific Understanding Be Assessed Through Drama?" *Primary Science Review* 45 (Dec): 4–5.

Marbach, E.S., and T.D. Yawkey. 1980. "The Effects of Imaginative Play Actions on Language Development in Five-Year-Old Children." *Psychology in the Schools* 17 (2): 257–263.

Musselwhite, C.R. 1986. "Using Signs as Gestural Cues for Children with Communicative Impairments." *Teaching Exceptional Children* 19 (1): 32–35.

National Association for the Education of Young Children. 1990. *Guidelines for Appropriate Curriculum Content and Assessment in Programs Serving Children Ages Three to Eight.* Washington, D.C.: NAEYC.

Osgood, C.E., G.J. Suci, and P.H. Tannenbaum. 1957. *The Measurement of Meaning.* Urbana: University of Illinois Press.

Ounce of Prevention Fund. 1996. *Starting Smart: How Early Experiences Affect Brain Development.* Chicago: Ounce of Prevention Fund.

Page, A. 1983. Children's Story Comprehension as a Result of Storytelling and Story Dramatization: A Study of the Child as Spectator and as Participant. Ph.D. diss., University of Massachusetts, Amherst.

Paley, V. 1990. *The Boy Who Would Be a Helicopter: The Use of Storytelling in the Classroom.* Cambridge, MA: Harvard University Press.

Patton, M.Q. 1987. *Creative Evaluation.* Newbury Park, CA: Sage Publications.

Pettigrew, J.C. 1994. "Drama: Slow Simmer or Rolling Boil?" *English in Texas* 26 (1): 26–28.

Phen, S., and R. Largon. 1981. "The Healing Mask." *Parabola* (6) August: 3.

Phillips, D.A., ed. 1987. *Quality in Child Care: What Does Research Tell Us?* Washington, D.C.: NAEYC.

Piaget, J. 1955/1974. *Language and Thought of the Child.* New York: Meridan-New American Library.

————.1962. *Play, Dreams, and Imitation in Early Childhood.* New York: Norton.

Piers, M.W., ed. 1972. *Play and Development: A Symposium with Contributions by Piaget and Others.* New York: W. W. Norton.

Pipkin, W., and S. DiMenna. 1989. "Using Creative Dramatics to Teach Conflict Resolution: Exploiting the Drama/Conflict Dialectic." *Journal of Humanistic Education and Development* 28 (2): 104–112.

Prothrow-Stith, D., and Quaday, S. 1995. *Hidden Casualties: The Relationship Between Violence and Learning.* National Health & Education Consortium and National Consortium for African American Children, Inc., Washington, D.C.

Robinson, S.P., and the National Educational Research Policy and Priorities Board. 1997. *Building Knowledge for a Nation of Learners: A Framework for Education Research 1997.* Washington, D.C.: U. S. Department of Education, Office of Educational Research and Improvement.

Salazar, L.G., G. Berghammer, V.L. Brown, and H. Griffin. 1993. "Social Pretend Play: An International Center for Studies in Theatre Education Technical Report." American Alliance for Theatre and Education.

Saldaña, J. 1995. *Drama of Color: Improvisation with Multiethnic Folklore.* Portsmouth, NH: Heinemann.

Saltz, E., and J. Johnson. 1977. "Training Disadvantaged Preschoolers on Various Fantasy Activities: Effects on Cognitive Functioning and Impulse Control." *Child Development* 48: 367–380.

Searle, J.R. 1983. *Intentionality.* Cambridge: Cambridge University Press.

Shipley, D. 1993. *Empowering Children: Play-based Curriculum for Lifelong Learning.* Scarborough, ON: Nelson Canada.

Slade, P. 1954. *Child Drama*. London: University of London Press.

Smilansky, S., and E. Klugman, eds. 1990. *Children's Play and Learning*. New York: Columbia University Press.

Smilansky, S., and L. Shefatya. 1990. *Facilitating Play: A Medium for Promoting Cognitive, Socioemotional, and Academic Development in Young Children*. Gaithersburg, MD: Psychosocial & Educational Publications.

Smith, D.O. 1991. "The Assessment Dilemma." In *Early Childhood Creative Arts: Proceedings of the International Early Childhood Creative Arts Conference, Los Angeles, CA*. L.Y. Overby, ed. 38–43. Reston, VA: National Dance Association.

Storr, A. 1983. *The Essential Jung*. Princeton, NJ: Princeton University Press.

Tucker, J.K. 1971. The Use of Creative Dramatics as an Aid in Developing Reading Readiness with Kindergarten Children. Ph.D. diss., University of Wisconsin, Madison.

Vygotsky, L. 1978. *Mind in Society: Development of Higher Psychological Process*. Cambridge, MA: Harvard University Press.

———. 1967. "Play and Its Role in the Mental Development of the Child." *Soviet Psychology* 12(6): 62–76.

Wagner, B.J. 1998. *Educational Drama and Language Arts: What Research Shows*. Portsmouth, NH: Heinemann.

Way, B. 1967. *Development Through Drama*. New York: Humanities Press.

Wittmer, D., and A. Honig. 1994. "Encouraging Positive Social Development in Young Children." *Young Children* 495: 4–12.

Wolf, S.A. 1996. "Language in and Around the Dramatic Curriculum." *Journal of Curriculum Studies* 27 (2): 117–137.